The Nepal Compact
Potential for Cold War II

By Bishnu Pathak, Ph.D.

Source: Susmita Bastola, 2022

Nepal Compact - Potential Cold War II   Bishnu Pathak, Ph.D.

Published by Cook Communication

1407 Getzelman Drive

Elgin, IL 60123

www.author-me.com

Not affiliated with Cook Communication Ministries

Cover Art and Frontispiece - Ms. Susmita Bastola

National Library of USA Cataloguing in Publication

ISBN
978-1-387-86020-3
Imprint: Lulu.com

Printed and bound in the USA

10 9 8 7 6 5 4 3 2 1

Table of Contents

The Nepal Compact

Potential for Cold War II

Bishnu Pathak, Ph.D.

Abstract

Nepal Compact is an integral part of the Millennium Challenge Corporation (MCC). The MCC is a grant agency established by the United States (US) to reduce global poverty. The objectives of the study are to: examine the cause and patterns; identify the grant areas, and evaluate controversial issues of the MCC. The state-of-the-art paper is prepared based upon literature review, archival research, and lesson-learned centric approach from yesterday, studies the axiomatic truth of the Nepal Compact today, and interprets how potential Cold War-II initiates from the geostrategic land Nepal tomorrow. The study method led to snowball techniques. The ratification of the Nepal Compact formally ended a chaotic five-year-long saga. But, its politico-diplomatic controversy spread in all tiers and professions even at the grassroots level. Large sections of Nepali people protest the assistance of the US and India in Nepal. There are many opportunities and a few are doubtful dilemmas in the MCC. A few controversial points of the Nepal Compact are: first, a senior US official disclosed the fact that MCC is a part of the Indo-Pacific Strategy (IPS). Second, nationalistic demagogy was orchestrated against the MCC because of China-affiliated communist forces and others. Third, owing to pros and cons, not only did the two-thirds Oli-led Communist fall but the CPN was also split into three factions. Fourth, the words investment and Americans interest are used in the MCC; in case of provisions of the MCC conflict with the Constitution and Nepali laws, the provisions of the MCC will be enforceable; Nepal needs to receive the consent of India on cross-border transmission line construction; the US could withdraw it unilaterally; intellectual property rights of the project would be with the US; and among others. Fifth, the US intended to include Nepal within its five strategic partners in the Indian Oceanic region. Sixth, ratifying to the MCC is against Nepal's foreign policy and China shall be furious with such decision of Nepal. Seventh, the Oli-led Government had a positive response to US' State Partnership Program under the IPS. Eight, the Compact grant has been the largest up-front partner started immediately after its establishment and it has not been succeeded everywhere, on the other. Last, no protocol was maintained during the entire process to till the MCC ratification. The US is also known as the country of guns and weapon industries. Owing to digital highways, jingoistic mediaism, and digital/cyber warfare, the illusion spread among the people that ratification of MCC means landed the US troops in Kathmandu as the air force aircraft landed three times in a year. Nepal is in between two giants Dragon (China) and Elephant (India). Nepal lies in a deep shadow between such emerging superpowers. The irony is that China is in a favor of a strong, stable, prosperous, and developed Nepal for one China policy whereas India desires to have a weak, poor, unstable, and underdeveloped country for the sake to control Nepal and its natural resources. Whether China and US-India develop cordial friendship, compete with one another, and live in a potential for Cold War II phase, Nepal will only be the victim. Unlike the world that was divided through ideological warfare in the Cold War I, the Cold War II potentially advances to being controlled by jingoistic mediaism, deluged by incongruous information. Cold War II will leave an impact on both global politico-media disillusionment and an internal psychological apparatus. There is saying, "The US does not do what it says; does not say what it does".

Keywords: MCC, Nepal Compact, Cold War II, Warfare, Freedom, India, China, and United States.

Prologue

This study by professor Bisnu Pathak is significant for many   reasons.

First, it is appropriate to congratulate Professor Bishnu for conducting such an exacting account of The Nepal Contract. His thorough historical research and scholarship underline the urgency regarding the situation in Nepal.

Second, Professor Bishnu is documenting a period when major world powers are competing for influence on weaker developing nations. Sadly, the purpose of these competitions may be seen as latter-day colonialism, even though history has proven the evils inherent in colonialism.

Third, the reader can see the dilemma of nations who need to ask for global assistance. Because of the competition between helpers, nations like Nepal are forced to choose between those who will help. Sadly, this choice can impact their   future   success   in   world   affairs.

We cannot ignore the similarity to problems Nepal faces in its border disputes with India. Or, worldwide, the problems faced by nations which have tried to help in Afghanistan, where nations came to "rescue" a nation. As in Afghanistan, a rescue can easily fail to achieve its goals. Often the help that came could only aid in the short term.

It is commendable that Professor Bishnu is faithfully documenting the Nepali Contract problem as it unfolds. Let us pray that Professor Bishnu's warning will stand as a safeguard against disaster for any of the countries - Nepal. China, and the United States.

---Bruce L. Cook, Ph.D.

Vice President/Co-Founder

Worldwide Peace Organization

Preface

There is a proverb in Nepal that is a saying, "Whoever white-black bull wins and loses by fighting in mustard fields, the damage would be tolerated by the poor peasant alone". This means that even if the US-led versus China-led alliance potentially advances for Cold War II owing to this MCC Nepal Compact ratification and other growing US-India vested interest reasons, the battleground would be Nepal only. Nepal cannot change or escape from two China and India's adjoining neighbors, but the US is a satellite friend. The world could not hold even a single COVID-19; one can only guess what will happen to Nepal if such a Cold War II situation arises. There is no doubt that the MCC is a part of the Indo-Pacific Strategy. Otherwise, the US would not have had to wait for 16 years (2006-2022) to get the MCC ratified by the House. The Nepal Compact must have been a contentious issue and long-awaited approval even in the history of US grants. The MCC controversy has spread from the center to the grassroots level in Nepal, on the one hand. On the other, permission is to be obtained from India for the transmission line construction. Even if the US and India look at Nepal with a single-door policy, it will not be anything other than a cosmetic relationship. Such Indo-US cosmetic relations will soon be broken once India realized that the US is also watching it from Nepalese land.

The Preamble of the MCC clearly states that it is an investment to enhance the American interest. The US has long carried out anti-Chinese activities within and beyond Nepalese land for dismantling and seceding the Chinese communist regime similar to the former Soviet Union in 1990. India is just behind the US to weaken China. To oust the communist regime from China, the US and its satellite alliance including India use jingoistic mediaism, whereas

7

China is far behind in such chauvinism because of the linguistic barrier. In this 21st century, media rules the entire world unlike '-ism', and '-logy'. The US-led war industries, oil companies, share markets, and drug and cigarette manufacturers are firmly entrenched in the world through tycoonism. Even the US President is not in a position to rule the world beyond the vested interests, advice, and even instructions of mediaism.

It is very easy for US or India to rule Nepal. The US adopts the strategy of

saam (motivation for the accomplishment),

daam (reward enough),

danda (punishment for not repeating), and

bhed (divide and rule) for the purposive works.

Nepal has a political and social culture of pursuing money. The US has a good understanding that they can often buy the concerned officials similar to commodities, goats available on market at a cheap price. As a result, there has been a huge discrepancy between the haves and haves not which is on the rise further. Nepal is sure to be further victimized owing to tug-of-warfare between US and China. It is unlikely to achieve the US desired result from the land of Nepal soon. That is why Nepal has the potential ground for Cold War II and that will continue for a long time too. Thus, the potential for Cold War II will beget further suffering in Nepal.

Bishnu Pathak, Nepal
pathakbishnu@gmail.com

Introduction

Nepal Compact is an integral part of the MCC. The MCC is an innovative and independent US foreign aid agency that helps to lead the fighting against global poverty (www.mcc.gov/about) and democratic human wrongs. The MCC is established by the US Congress for bilateral support in 2004. It selects the countries that meet certain specifications to provide grants. It delivers time-limited grants stimulating economic growth, reducing poverty, and consolidating institutions. It speaks, "These investments not only support stability and prosperity in partner countries but also enhance American interests" (www.mcc.gov/about).

The MCC Board uses four-step processes: identify candidate country, establish selection methodology, publish country scorecards, and select country (www.mcc.gov/who-we-select/selection-process). It invests to: create jobs and expand markets, build a more stable world, promote growth through infrastructure, invest in the next generation, incentivize policy and institutional reform, empower women and girls, increase the capacity of partner governments, to give entrepreneurs tools to succeed, and lay the groundwork for healthy communities (www.mcc.gov/about). It has decided to provide 51 compacts for 35 countries, as of 2022 (www.mcc.gov/where-we-work).

On February 27, 2022, the US Government's MCC $500 million Compact with the Government of Nepal was ratified along with interpretive declarations despite huge controversies among the great populace in Nepal. An additional $130 million is to be contributed by the Government of Nepal. The Nepal compact aims to maintain road quality, increase the accessibility and consistency of electricity, and facilitate cross-border energy trade between

Nepal and India that helps to spur investments, accelerate economic growth, and reduce poverty (www.mcc.gov/news-and-events/podcast/episode-033122-nepal-compact-ratification).

The Nepal Compact was ratified by the House of Representatives during a period when Nepal's economy was being struggled with a liquidity crisis in all commercial banks (September 2021 to April 2022), low capital expenditure, and declined remittances. The country's total debt has enlarged from 20.6 percent during the fiscal year of 2016–2017 to 40.72 percent in the fiscal year of 2020–2021 (Public Debt Management Office, 2021). Even though, the Compact's ratification raises numbers of vertical to horizontal interpretations from center, region, district, and grassroots levels. These diverging arguments and interpretations belong to development, sovereignty, geopolitics, security, and governance which are no less than politico-economic warfare.

The MCC process began in 2006 when Nepal received the first official letter of invitation from the MCC Headquarters. It took 11 years to sign the agreement in September 2017. It was signed as an unequal protocol status by Finance Minister on behalf of Nepal and the Acting CEO of MCC similar to the Joint Secretary of Government of Nepal. Moreover, it took 16 years for its ratification by the House of Representatives. It was the first time in Nepal's history that it took so a long period to accept such a grant. The first reason for this was that a small number of people with thin voices were in favor to approve the MCC. On the other hand, the number of those who were against the ratification of it was a strong, logical, and loud voice. Owing to sharp controversies and criticism, the two-thirds majority holding the then PM K P Oli-led Government of the Communist Party of Nepal was ousted in three and a half years and the party also split into three factions: CPN (UML), CPN (Maoist Center), and CPN (Unified Socialist). In the meantime, the US continued to put pressure on Nepal and Nepalese leaders. The US Assistant Secretary Donald Lu also warned the major parties' top leaders including the Nepalese PM to face the consequences of disapproval of the Compact and severely humiliated all other top leaders.

The term Cold War I is a state of warfare that occurs between the countries due to differing ideological thoughts. This means it is a matter of politico-ideological warfare than direct military actions between two the US-Soviet Union blocs and their satellite followers of the nations. The Cold War I had been warfare between capitalist versus communist blocs of satellite rulings that had held the span of the Truman Doctrine started in March 1947 and ended along with the dissolution of the Soviet Union in December 1991 (Service, 2015). This is no less than an episode of proxy warfare (Osmańczyk, 2002; Hughes, 2014; & Williams, 2012) between the two superpowers, the USA and the Soviet Union.

The US's greatest and clandestine plan is seceding Tibet to make China a weak, vulnerable, and identity-based conflicting country. The most suitable country for the seceding purpose cannot be any other than geostrategic and porous Nepal. Despite the long duration and political turmoil in Nepal, the MCC has been ratified, unlike BRI's agreement alone. The chronological details 1 to 4 tables are self-evident of how much the US is interested to ratify the MCC in Nepal. On the other hand, China is also putting all-around pressure on the leaders and security forces through telephonic conversations and making frequent visits to Nepal to prevent the US's policy of encircling China from Nepal. These trends are no less than the initiation of Cold War II, mainly from the land of Nepal. Thus, Cold War II is a state of warfare between competing nations through politico-economic, psycho-social/cultural, and espionage warfare, propaganda as a proxy, and satellite wars waged by the USA and China, liberal democrats vs hard liner people's democrats. Cold War I had been ideological warfare whereas Cold War II belongs to identity-based warfare/chauvinistic mediaism, monopolizing the US-desired war industries, and liquefied natural gas market in the world.

Warfare is a normal course of economic, socio-cultural, information, and politico-legal proxy war (Pathak, 2015) than the direct visible military fighting. The world's powerful USA alliance secretly adopts economic, administrative, diplomatic, espionage, propaganda, and tactical methods, procedures, and mechanisms to weaken their rival China, and its satellite grouping is called warfare in this paper. Warfare is itself less humanity, showing muscle of superiority. The Cold War II leads to mediaism and digital-cyber warfare rather than physical fighting.

This paper aims to describe the Nepal Compact by investigating the axiomatic truth of MCC that occurred within Nepal after the Oli-led Government decided to submit it to the Secretariat of the House of Representatives for its ratification.   The aim refers to illustrate the chronological details amid many ups and downs in which the Nepal Compact was initiated, prepared, accepted, and signed between the two nations. It further aims to articulate easing to the faculty members, research scholars, professionals, students, and policymakers. The debates and fear began in favor and against the Nepal Compact after adding a provision of its 'ratification' that has not been a part of the MCC agreement signed in Washington in 2017. Nepal, which is sandwiched, should not be a battleground owing to the imposition of the BRI (Belt and Road Initiative) and MCC.

The General Objective of this study is to interpret the process of initiation, preparation, acceptance, and signature of the MCC and to provide the rights information on what the MCC is and for what purpose it works for all concerned and interested individual parties. It is attempted to address the pervasive concern whether the Cold War II is being initiated by geo-strategic important country Nepal which has signed the BRI, a few months before the MCC agreement.

The Specific Objective is to examine and evaluate the complete cause, nature, degree, and patterns of the MCC Nepal Compact that has been signed-ratified by Nepal for the purpose to accelerate economic growth and reducing poverty; to find out the areas where Compact grant uses in Nepal; to analyze why MCC has become so controversial within and beyond Nepal; and to interpret the possible future scenario of Nepal in five years of its implementation and thereafter.

This paper followed an interpretive research method that comprehended some of the interpretations raised in the course of ratification of the MCC Nepal Compact at the International and all tiers of Nepal. This state-of-the-art paper is analyzed based on the archival research literature of various publication houses along with the author's notebook, lessons-learned centric approach, and participant observation following the modus operandi of networking tracking method or snowball techniques (Pathak, 2020). Information is gathered through printed books, journals, reports, and newspapers. Experts' view or opinion is also included. The pioneering paper briefly adopts victim-centric or reader-friendly approaches to reviewing the whole critiques and or controversies of the Nepal Compact. To accomplish the task, the author follows an inductive study method. Rather than generalizing an existing theoretical framework, it pursues a new Human Security paradigm encompassing "freedom" approaches similar to universal-natural fundamental rights (Pathak, September 2013).

Human security is a general phenomenon that applies everywhere poor to rich and individuals to all people in the world. Human security is a security of all dimensions; human, state to nature in the universe (Pathak, 2014). Human security is a comprehensive, interrelated, and interconnected conceptual approach. It is a very important issue for all human beings that is needed in their homes, in their jobs, in their schools, and nature to comfortably live, grow, play, study, work, and enjoy (Pathak, 2013). It is a broad notion, protection from military to non-State and natural-manmade disasters. Human security states to people-nature and pro-biology-centered notion, whereas human rights are human-centered more (Pathak, 2014). It is a comprehensive, interrelated, and coordinated concept that encompasses freedom from want, freedom from fear, freedom to live in dignity, freedom to take action on one's behalf, and freedom to inherit a pro-nature and pro-biology environment for forthcoming generations as inherent, non-alienable, and fundamental rights (Pathak, August 2013). On the other side, one of the core concepts of MCC is freedom of hunger free society too.

The paper is further categorized into six subheadings, namely:

- freedom to establish power-centric politics,
- freedom of unilateral declaration rights,
- freedom for the formation of the fighting ring,
- freedom for arguments
- freedom from China's scary, and
- freedom on the empire of a lie.

The categorization is carried out following the universality, indivisibility, interconnectedness, interdependence, and interrelatedness as well as the imposition of Cold War II as an advanced experiment from small, landlocked, weak, poor, defenseless, sandwiched, and conflicting country Nepal. On the advancement of Cold War II, the US will have minimal losses, while India will have some losses, but China will suffer a lot. In this entire intriguing situation, Nepal will continuously be a tug of war between the US versus China.

Freedom to establish power-centric politics

Nepali politics has been used as a social service along with the volunteering concept at the beginning of the restoration of democracy in 1990 is transformed into a full-fledged profession, furthermore, as *pewa* (personal belongings or property). Except for a rare case, no matter how much any academia has contributed for the sake of the nation and people staying at home (without going abroad) country, he had/has not been or will not be able to hold any position without being a bag carrier of the political party or leader. Even in such recruitments, history has been a witness that only a leader's puppet-one has got a position excluding honest and common activists. Owing to the absence of political ideologies, the top leaders even within the party have been carrying the bags of North, South, and West countries with ambitions to continuously stay in power or grasp the sate-power.

A well-known scholar Ananda Aditya says, "The USA values our strategic space, China seeks stake building" (February 20, 2022) in Nepal. This means that India, the United States, and China desired to make Nepal a shadow country or puppet nation through their physical presence in the various projects including the MCC and BRI. Such competition to make Nepal on their fold invites in many cases digital warfare too. Such a power tussle to minimize the role of China in global politics from the land of Nepal can also consider the beginning or potential of Cold War II. There has been a great influence and debate having the implementation of the MCC in Nepal rather than BRI proposals. The concept of the MCC was developed to address Millennium Development Goals to minimize poverty and hunger.

The Millennium Development Goals (MDGs) had been established by the Millennium Summit of the United Nations in 2000 following the adoption of the UN Millennium Declaration (A/RES/55/2). These were developed based on the OECD DAC International Development Goals which were agreed upon by Development Ministers in shaping the 21st Century Strategy in May 1996 (DAC-OECD, May 1996). All 195 UN member states and at least 22 international organizations expressed their commitment to achieve the Millennium Development Goals by 2015, which focussed for eradicate extreme poverty and hunger, achieving universal primary education, promoting gender equality, empowering women, reducing child mortality, improving maternal health, combat HIV/AIDS, malaria, and other diseases, to ensure environmental sustainability, and global partnership   for   development (research.un.org/en/docs/dev/2000-2015).

Former Finance Minister Ram Saran Mahat writes that the MCC assists the UN General Assembly's declaration of MDG in 2000 to achieve the goals in the developing countries through development aid targeting to combat poverty, hunger, disease, illiteracy, infrastructure development, environmental degradation, gender equality, and human rights for the promotion of living standards of human beings (August 26, 2021).

Mahat represented Nepal at the UN International Conference 2002 on Development Finance in Monterrey, Mexico where heads of the International Organizations including the UN, World Bank, International Monetary Fund, World Trade Organisation, and over 50 heads of State or Government along with 200 ministers participated. He recalls, "Addressing the conference, US President

George Bush committed to raising US development assistance by 50 percent with an additional US Dollar 5 billion annually through millennium challenge accounts (MCA). Subsequently, the MCC was established by the US Congress in January 2004 as a foreign aid agency for bipartisan aid to promote economic growth and poverty reduction and strengthen institutions" (August 26, 2021). Its sole purpose is to provide financial assistance in a manner that promotes economic growth and the elimination of extreme poverty and strengthens good governance, economic freedom, and investments in people (Millennium Challenge Act, 2003).

When King Gyanendra Shah ended his direct ruling regime by reinstating the dissolved House of Representatives in Nepal on April 24, 2006 (BBC News, April 24, 2006), the following day, Girija Prasad Koirala re-appointed Prime Minister of Nepal, the Chair of the country's largest party Nepali Congress, on behalf of Seven Parliamentary Party Alliance (The New York Times, April 25, 2006). Its main purpose was to end the decade-long People's War, rewrite the country's Constitution through Constituent Assembly, and either reduce the king's power or even eliminate the monarchy forever declaring Republic Nepal.

Immediate after the reestablishment of democratic government, the then Finance Minister Mahat appealed to the international communities to financially assist Nepal. A couple of months later, Nepal received the first official letter from the MCC Headquarters and invited Nepal's representatives to hold a meeting with them in Washington to study MCC's fiscal management threshold status in 2006.

The threshold phase of MCC was approved for Nepal in December 2011. Based on Nepal's commitment to its MCC policy indicators, the Board of Directors of MCC selected

Nepal as eligible to develop a compact, a larger grant-based investment (Press Statement, July 21, 2017).

After MCC selected Nepal for a smaller threshold program in December 2011 (Acharya, September 16, 2017), the MCC and the Government of Nepal analyzed Nepal's constraints to economic growth and jointly prepared a policy improvement program based on the results. Given Nepal's strong performance on its MCC policy indicator scorecard through 2014, the MCC's Board of Directors selected Nepal as eligible to develop a Nepal Compact in the field of Electricity Transmission and Road Maintenance Projects, a larger grant-based investment.

The energy component comprises a 400 kV power transmission line to expand inside Nepal from Lapsifedi, (Kathmandu) to Damauli and Hetauda and Nepal to a second cross-border transmission line from Butwal (Sunal) to Gorakhpur, India (Nepal Compact, September 2017). The road maintenance includes Mechi, Koshi, and Sagarmatha highways, among others (Nepal Compact, September 2017). Finally, on September 14, 2017, Finance Minister Gyanendra Bahadur Karki and Jonathan Nash, Acting Chief Executive Officer of the MCC, signed the pact in Washington. The brief detailed processes have been given in Chronological Details 1.

Chronological Details1: Initial Preparation, Preparation, Continuation, and Acceptance of the Compact		
Step	Particular	Date
1	Proclamation of Millennium Challenge Act	2003
2	Nepal received its first official letter from the MCC Headquarters	2006
3	Nepal formally requested the MCC grant	January 2010
4	MCC selected Nepal as eligible	December

	for a $500 million grant	2011
5	MCC selected Nepal to continue developing threshold programs in 2013	December 19, 2012
6	MCC and Nepal conducted a diagnostic study in Nepal	2013-2014
7	MCC Board voted for Nepal to make eligible for the Compact	December 10, 2014
8	MCC opened its office in Kathmandu, Nepal	April 2015
9	Nepal was reselected by the MCC Board	December 17, 2015
10	MCC conducted feasibility studies from 2016 to 2017	November 2016
11	MCC Board approved Nepal Compact Program ($500 million grant)	August 17, 2017
12	Agreement signed between the Ministry of Finance, Nepal, and MCC	September 14, 2017
Source: Author's notebook		

When the MCC agreement was signed on September 14, 2018, there was no provision for its approval by Parliament. On February 10, 2019, the Ministry of Finance put forward the Nepal Compact agreement to the Federal Parliament for its approval referring to the decision of the Council of Ministers. Earlier, responding to the request from the Ministry of Finance on December 28, 2018, the Secretary of the Ministry of Law decided on January 10, 2019, that the Compact was to be approved by the House of Representatives. Even today, there is widespread concern that why such a controversial decision of the Compact was made by the Secretary without the approval of the Law Minister.

The letter which was signed by Arjun Bhusal of the Law Ministry says, "As the opinion of the Ministry of Finance has been sought in this regard, as per the provisions of the Nepal Treaty Act 1990, to make effective the provision mentioned in Article 7 of the Nepal Compact that 'if the law of Nepal conflicts with the provisions of the agreement, the agreement will be used, the Compact has to be approved by a simple majority of the House of Representatives'" (Himalkhabar, February 26, 2022). The Ministry claimed that the ratification decision was taken as they were instructed by the then PM Oli.

The Oli-led Government registered Nepal Compact in Parliament on July 15, 2019, for its ratification (Post Report, February 20, 2022, & Ranjan, September 20, 2021), but did not dare to table it in the House of Representatives because of sharp conflict and vertical division within the CPN.

On February 2, 2020, a three-member Task Force was formed by the ruling communist party headed by Ex-Prime Minister Jhalanath Khanal comprising CPN Vice-President Bhim Rawal and the then Foreign Minister Pradip Gyawali. In three weeks, the agreement greatly left impacts on national sovereignty and the freedom of Nepal and the Nepali people, Khanal's team recommended to the Oli-led Government not to ratify the Nepal Compact agreement without revising some of the 'objectionable provisions' on it (Sharma, February 22, 2020, Online Khabar, February 22, 2020, & Pradhan, February 21, 2020). Stating delaying ratification is delaying the benefits, on June 29, 2020, the US Embassy in Kathmandu states, "Accepting this grant is Nepal's choice but the availability of the funding is not open-ended" (US Embassy in Nepal, June 29, 2020). Chronological Details 2 gives a brief understanding of the activities of the Nepal Compact.

	Chronological Details 2: Exercises to the approval of the MCC by Parliament under Oli's leadership	
Step	**Particular**	**Date**
1	Seeking opinion from the Ministry of Finance to the Ministry of Law	December 28, 2018
2	Nepal Compact to be approved by a simple majority	January 10, 2019
3	The Govt. submitted the MCC Agreement to the House for ratification	February 8, 2019
4	Government registered Compact at the Parliamentary Secretariat	July 15, 2019
5	Implementation agreement signed between Finance Minister and MCC	September 29, 2019
6	CPN Standing Committee directed Govt. to seek clarity by MCC Board	December 21, 2019
7	Chinese Ambassador to Nepal welcomed any economic support to Nepal	January 3, 2020
8	Ruling CPN formed a three members Task Force led by ex-PM Khanal	February 2, 2020
9	Khanal led Task Force submitted Report to both chairs of the CPN	February 21, 2020
10	US Embassy in Nepal said availability to MCC grant is not open-ended	June 29, 2020
11	Nepal requested to MCC Headquarters to extend its deadline	June 29, 2020
Source: Author's notebook		

The US Department of State Secretary Antony J. Blinken spoke with Nepali Prime Minister Sher Bahadur Deuba on July 27, 2021, while he had been on an official visit to India. Blinken's telephone call could bring Nepal closer to the United States. Such talks may not have a significant impact on Kathmandu's relations with Beijing (Post Reporter, July 27, 2021).

On September 9, 2021, the MCC Vice President Fatema Sumar arrived in Kathmandu to discuss the required next steps to implement the grant infrastructure program, address the clarification questions provided by Nepal, and hear from the people of Nepal. The US Embassy Media note stated that the grant program does not have a military component and that will not impede Nepal's sovereignty, and Nepal's constitution will prevail over the agreement. PM Deuba and CPN (Maoist Center) Dahal sent a joint letter to MCC Headquarters setting a deadline of February 28, 2022 (Annex-I). The Fatema-led delegation met PM Deuba, former PMs Oli and Prachanda among other senior officials (Republica, September 12, 2021).

Again on December 19, 2020, a three-member task force team was headed by Khanal to study the contentious points of the MCC and the team will provide suggestions after in-depth studies and discussions (Sharma, December 20, 2021). But the team could not materialize its work and tenure due to PM Deuba and Nepali Congress being uninterested in further studies on the disputed issues under the pressure of the United States (for furthermore, please follow chronological details 3). History has been a witness that PM Deuba affiliated and even in many cases protected, uplifted by the US Government. The US played a pivotal role to oust the Oli-led communist government and to establishing pro-American government headed by Deuba. The Chronological Details 3 provides discussions for Nepal Compact ratification.

Chronological Details 3: Discussions on the process of Nepal Compact ratification		
Step	**Particular**	**Date**
1	During US Secretary Antony Blinken's visit to India, there had been a telephone conversation with PM Deuba on the Nepal Compact	July 27, 2021
2	Nepal sent an 11-point letter to the MCC HQs for its clarification	September 3, 2021
3	MCC Headquarters sent 13-page long clarification	September 8, 2021
4	MCC team led by Fatima Sumar's official visit in Nepal	Sep. 9-12, 2021
5	Sumar briefed her MCC Board having Compact's discussions	September 29, 2021
6	PM Deuba and CPN (Maoist Center) Dahal sent a joint letter to MCC Headquarters setting a deadline of February 28, 2022	September 29, 2021
7	Nepal private business sector pressures Govt. to ratify the MCC	October 7, 2021
8	MCC statement on the Nepal Compact	October 29, 2021
9	PM Deuba met Deputy CEO Ms Alexia Latortue in Glasgow, Scotland	November 2, 2021
10	PM Deuba publicly said Dahal and he sent a joint letter to the MCC	November 4, 2021
11	Dahal refuted Deuba's claim	November 5, 2021
12	Donald Lu, US Assistant Secretary of State Affairs visited Nepal	Nov. 18-19, 2021

13	The House Session was called two weeks earlier than the usual schedule	December 14, 2021
14	MCC Board of Directors urged Nepal to ratify MCC soon	December 15, 2021
15	Govt. formed a three-member Compact led by former PM Khanal	December 19, 2021
Source: Author's notebook		

After a long tug-of-war among the mainstream parties, the Deuba-led government tabled the MCC at the Parliament Secretariat on February 20, 2022. The main opposition UML had been obstructing the parliament for the past six months in protest of the Speaker's decision not to dismiss the UML expelled lawmakers. It means, the Compact was tabled in the House amidst UML parliamentarians' obstruction and slogans. Against the MCC tabulation, conscious people voluntarily came to the streets and were protesting with police batons, boots, and water fountains in front of the parliament building. Parliamentarians including Dev Gurung, chief whip of the CPN (Maoist Center), Bhim Rawal, leader of the CPN-UML, Prem Suwal, Nepal Mazdoor Kisan Party, and Durga Poudel of the Rashtriya Janamorcha had protested within Parliamentary discussion against the MCC's move. Even the Speaker of the House of Representatives was against the ratification of the Compact. The author tried to write a brief note here stating what happened surrounding Kathmandu just before and after the MCC was tabled in the House and ratified accordingly.

On February 10, 2022, US Assistant Secretary of State Donald Lu held telephone conservations with the top three leaders of mainstream political parties, namely PM Sher Bahadur Deuba, K P Oli, Chair of the CPN (UML), and Prachanda, Chair of the CPN (Maoist Center) (Khabarhub,

February 10, 2022). Lu phoned and asked PM Deuba to ratify the Nepal Compact from the Federal Parliament within the stipulated deadline of February 28, 2022. Lu warned Oli, stating, "MCC should be ratified. It would not good for you if you did not ratify it. The provision to ratify the Compact from the House was decided by the cabinet headed by PM Oli. This project was put forward in agreement with you". Threatening Prachanda, Lu stated, "First you have to make a quick decision, 'yes' or 'no' on the ratification of the MCC. Second, the provisions of the Nepal Compact will not be amended. Third, time will not be added further. Fourth, if you do not accept the grant, it is up to you, but the US takes it seriously. Fifth, if the MCC could not approve on stipulated time, the US confirms that it happened because of China" (Sharma, February 11, 2022). He warned all of the top three leaders of Nepal stating that Washington will review its relations if Nepal failed to ratify the Nepal Compact.

On February 11, 2022, Kantipur daily publishes a story about how a provision not included in the MCC agreement of September 14, 2017, was added to be ratified by the Parliament during Oli's tenure. In September 2017, a Nepali team led by the then Finance Minister Gyanendra Bahadur Karki reached Washington to hold talks with the US officials for an agreement of the MCC. There had been intense talks for three days for negotiation while the US officials put forward the agenda, an "agreement to be passed by Nepal's Parliament". But, Nepal's officials questioned, "Since dozens of projects receive grants from dozens of countries every year, why did this agreement only have to be ratified by the parliament?" After many deliberations on such a contentious issue, the US agreed to sign the agreement without the need for parliamentary ratification. On February 8, 2019, on the recommendation of Finance Minister Yubaraj Khatiwada, the cabinet meeting headed by PM KP Oli decided to ratify the MCC through the Federal Parliament (Pandey, February 12, 2022), under pressure and influence of the US.

On the other hand, former ambassadors, political leaders, civil society, etc. protested against the languages, warnings, and reviews used by the US Assistant Secretary of State with the top three leaders. Having such intimidating language used by Lu, all concerned professional officials stated that such initiatives will badly hurt bilateral, economic, political, military, and diplomatic relations with the US in the future (Pandey, February 12, 2022).

On February 14, 2014, the statement of the US Embassy in Kathmandu refuted reports of threatening Nepali top leaders concerning the issue of the MCC Compact. A statement says, "It is false", but we are asking Nepal to follow through on its commitments". It further says, "After years of delays on following through on Nepal's promise, we simply ask that ratifying the agreement be brought to a vote so the people, through their elected officials have their say. We have had discussions with Nepali leaders – but not in the way characterized by some press and online discourse" (Khabarhub, March 14, 2022). What happened during the ratification processes is mentioned in the Chronological Details 4 briefly.

Chronological Details 4: In the midst of many ups and downs, Nepal ratified the Compact		
Step	**Particular**	**Date**
1	MCC HQ made public a joint letter sent by PM Deuba and Prachanda	February 3, 2022
2	MCC Acting CEO sent a warning letter to PM Deuba and Prachanda	February 3, 2022
3	US Assistant Secretary Donald Lu separately warned to PM Deuba, Oli, and Prachanda by phone.	February 10, 2022
4	Public agitation on streets against the ratification of the Nepal Compact	Feb. 10-27, 2022
5	Chinese Foreign Ministry Spokesperson said, "China opposes US coercive diplomacy" to Nepal to ratify the Nepal Compact grant	February 18, 2022
6	Nepal Compact tabled in the Secretariat of the Federal Parliament	February 20, 2022
7	The House session ratified the MCC Compact Nepal	February 27, 2022
8	A 12-point interpretative declaration was endorsed by the House	February 27, 2022
9	US welcomed the ratification	March 1, 2022
10	Nepal voted for UN Resolution against the Russian invasion of Ukraine	March 3, 2022
11	US Embassy in Kathmandu denied threatening to top Nepalese leaders	March 14, 2022

12	A US Air Force aircraft landed at Kathmandu Airport third time in a year	March 18, 2022
13	US Embassy said, "MCC ratification is Nepal's sovereign decision"	March 19, 2022
14	Nepal voted at UNGA against the humanitarian crisis in Ukraine	March 24, 2022
15	Three day Nepal visit of Chinese Foreign Minister/State Councilor	March 25-27, 2022
16	A three-day official visit of a four US Congressional Delegation, headed by Senator Kristen Jillibrand to Nepal	April 22-24, 2022
17	US Under Secretary Uzra Zeya, Tibetan Refugees leader arrived in Kathmandu	May 20-22, 2022
18	Commanding General of the United States Army Pacific Charles Flynn arrived in Kathmandu	June 9-12, 2022
Source: *Author's notebook*		

Nepali Congress, CPN (Maoist Center), CPN (Unified Socialist), and Janata Socialist Party (JSP). Differences within the coalition were also widening. The Maoist Center has decided not to ratify the MCC in the status quo. The party had decided to leave the government if the MCC ratification process was put forward by force. The Unified Socialist was also not in a position to ratify MCC in the status quo. They said, "Let's try to modify it. Let's ask for them what the reason for not accepting amendment is. One of the options is to get them to write a letter of explanation. Resolving by consensus is another option" (Sharma and Neupane, February 16, 2022). The Nepali Congress was trying to persuade the alliance. But, PM Deuba was also discussing alternatives of it with UML.

On February 16, Prachanda inserted pressure on PM Deuba to be patient for consensus stating that no one in the party was ready to ratify the Compact. The Maoist parliamentary party had decided to leave the government if the MCC was tabled. Even though, PM Deuba-his party was ready to wait for a couple of days at the coalition partners' request. Nepali Congress had already decided to make a final decision (ratify or not) tabling the Compact in the Parliament (Annapurna Post, February 16, 2022). On the other hand, Deuba initiated the process of indirect (informal and formal) and direct (informal and formal) talks with the UML. The UML had a vested desire to break the alliance first and form the government under Oli's leadership. Under the conspiratorial game theory and to insert the pressure on coalition partners, PM Deuba formally asked UML to participate in the Government under his leadership on February 17, 2022.

Wang Wenbin, Chinese Foreign Ministry Spokesperson opposed "coercive diplomacy," of the US to Nepal on the course to ratify the Nepal Compact. This statement was proclaimed during a press conference held in Beijing on February 18 (Wenbin, February 18, 2022). On February 10, 2022, US Assistant Secretary Donald Lu held or warned that Washington would review its ties with Nepal (Annapurna Express, February 18, 2022) if the MCC failed to ratify by the House.

On February 20, the Compact grant agreement was tabled in the House of Representatives. Prachanda and Madhav Kumar Nepal agreed to table for ratification, but senior fellow leaders objected to them. Activists except Nepali Congress were protesting on the streets. And clashes were occurring between protestors versus security forces where a man was killed and dozens of others were injured. PM

Deuba continued to hold discussions with the ruling party alliance and the main opposition UML party to reach a majority for the Nepal Compact.

On February 22, Deuba was in constant dialogue to get the UML involved in the Nepal Compact ratification process. But Oli unremittingly insisted that the UML could only have participated in the discussion process once PM Deuba broke the coalition alliance. Deuba did not dare to break the alliance as he has become a fifth-time PM with the full fledge cooperation by the alliance.

On February 23, the two sides' leaders of the alliance were awaiting each other's final step at the crucial time for the MCC agreement to be ratified by the Federal Parliament. Coalition government partners who had been trying to dissuade and exhaust their fellow travelers were then frustrated with each other. PM Deuba had only one expectation from the ruling coalition partners: the Maoists and the Unified Socialists, to be boycotted during the ratification process. But the Maoist and Socialist leaders had already decided to present in parliament and vote against the Compact ratification. Deuba had made clear that the alliance will break down and he would ask for cooperation with the UML. For this, various Congress leaders had continued dialogue with UML leaders. The alliance was on the verge of breaking up immediately once the UML supported PM Deuba. However, the UML had not been clear about supporting the Deuba government.

On February 24, there had been intense discussions between the Nepali Congress and UML to continue the Deuba Government till holding all tiers of elections and to ratify the MCC from the Parliament. They also agreed to bring an impeachment motion against the Maoist Speaker and agreed to share Governments in provinces. It seemed that the alliance had broken down and a formal announcement of it was very close. PM Deuba and UML

Oli had group discussions at the Parliament House in Baneshwor in the morning and a one-and-one meeting in Baluwatar in the evening. They were much closed to an agreement to oust the coalition partners.

But a (power-centric) dramatic twist started to happen to owe by the active role of mid-tier of coalition leaders on February 25. They were engaged to identify a new path of discussions with restraint. Two options liked either to ratify the agreement through interpretative declaration or stay in the absence of Maoist and Socialist parliamentarians during the Nepal Compact voting in the Parliament. After the Nepal Congress-UML concluding talks, the Maoists and the Socialists were great under pressure. Several indirect (informal and formal) and direct (informal and formal) meetings were also held to discuss the pros and cons once the alliance broke down. Finally, Prachanda and Madhav Nepal tried hard to continue the alliance seeking the middle path.

Finally, three-coalition government leaders, namely, Deuba, Prachanda, and Nepal agreed to ratify the compact through an interpretative declaration by Parliament earlier on February 27, 2022. The compact agreement was ratified by a unanimous vote of the House of Representatives on the same day. The agreement was approved as per the agreement reached between the ruling Nepali Congress, the CPN (Maoist Center), and the CPN (Unified Socialist).

A four-member delegation of the Lower and Upper Houses of the US Congress had been on a three-day visit to Nepal. A high-level delegation was led by Senator Kirsten Gillibrand including Senators Sheldon Whitehouse, Cory Booker, and Mark Kelly, and visited (April 22-24, 2022) in Nepal on the course to enforce the US policies in Nepal. They discussed a wide range of issues from bilateral economic assistance and cooperation such as Tibetan refugees, the MCC compact, and Nepal's position on the

Russia-Ukraine conflict (New Spotlight Online, April 23, 2022). This 2022 year, both the US-Nepal celebrate the 75th anniversary of official diplomatic ties.

Nepalis have been in the habit of abusing or rebuking America for a long time. We remain silent about who our party leaders are. America always works for its country and people. If Nepal had been dear to our Nepali leaders, such a situation would never be invited. Due to the strategic space given by the leaders to the US, the US came to Nepal with the proposal of the Nepal Compact grant keeping Nepal as the first and top priority. It took 16 years to ratify from the House. The United States has much waited to play in such a geo-strategic important place Nepal. Rather than rebuking other countries like the US, let's sit together to develop the good character, moral, visionary, honest, and socialist leaders who can keep Nepal, people, and good professionals at the center similar to Americans. Let's not become the bag-carrying cadres alone of the leaders avaricious of what leaders give.

It is unappreciated to rebuke and blame foreign countries like the US alone. If they had a strong notion and clear vision to develop a prosperous nation despite the jealousy and greed to attain power and self-property only to their own, family, relatives, and a section of their courtiers even within the party, the foreign forces never get an opportunity to play a conspiratorial game from Nepal. It happened because leaders are always associated with a favorable country. For example, the top three leaders namely PM Deuba, Oli, and Prachanda are affiliated with the US, India, and China respectively. They put their masters at the top priority rather than the people and nation. Thus, Nepali leaders are the prime ones responsible to create potential warfare of Cold War II.

Freedom of unilateral declaration rights

Unilateral is a decision taken by only one side of a specific country, institution, and group. It is involved in a particular situation before bi-or-tri- or multilateral agreement or ratification. Clause 1.2 of the UN Law Commission Report says that an interpretative declaration is a unilateral statement where the State purports to specify/clarify the meaning/scope of a treaty or of certain of its provisions (Ghimire, February 28, 2022). In a few cases, interpretative declarations were also held before the ratification of the treaty of agreement. The declaration is a formal explicit announcement. A declaration defines a statement made by a concerned party to a legal transaction usually not under oath   (www.merriam-webster.com/dictionary/declaration). Every state has a right to accept or reject any treaty or agreement following good conduct, truth, and justice putting the people and nation first.

The 12-point interpretative declaration was adopted by the Cabinet and ratified by the House of Representatives on February 27, 2022, along with the Millennium Challenge Corporation Nepal Compact.

Among the declarations, Nepal can cancel the compact unilaterally by providing 30 days' notice if the project is seen as against Nepalese law. The interpretative declaration stated that Nepal has not joined any arms and ammunition, military, or security alliance despite its cooperation in the MCC development project. The interpretative declarations are:

1.   Nepal declares that by being a party to the Compact, Nepal shall not be a party to any US strategic, military, or security alliance, including the Indo-Pacific Strategy.

2.   Nepal declares that the Constitution of Nepal, being the fundamental law of the land, shall prevail over the Compact and other associated agreements.

3.   Concerning Section 2.7, Section 5.1 (iii) 5.1 (b) (iv) of the Compact, the Nepali government understands that these sections are intended to apply only to the use of the MCC funding and program assets and that the provisions do not and shall not obligate Nepal to comply with the current or future United States' laws and policies for any purpose other than the use of the MCC funding.

4.   Concerning Section 3.2 (b) of the Compact, Nepal declares that the conduct of activities of the Millennium Challenge Account Nepal Development Board (the MCA Nepal) shall be governed by the laws of Nepal and regulated by provisions of the compact.

5.   Concerning Section 3.2 (f) of the Compact, Nepal declares that MCC will not have ownership of the intellectual property and that Nepal shall own and fully enjoy all the intellectual property created under the Compact program.

6.   Concerning Section 3.5, Nepal declares that implementation letters under the Compact shall be implemented within the scope of the Compact.

7.   Concerning Section 3.8(a) of the compact, Nepal declares that in addition, the audits of all activities and funds of MCA Nepal shall be audited by the Office of the Auditor General following the prevailing laws of Nepal.

8.   Concerning Section 5.1(a) of the Compact, Nepal declares that in addition to Nepal's right to terminate the Compact without cause by giving 30 days prior written

either side notice, Nepal has the right to terminate the Compact by giving 30 days prior written notice in case the activities/ programs under the compact violate Nepal's laws or policies.

9.   Concerning Section 5.5 of the Compact, Nepal declares that provisions under the Compact that survive after the expiration, suspension, or termination of the Compact shall only relate to the compact program and the use of MCC funding, including for the evaluation of the projects under the Compact, audits, and settlements of taxes.

10.   Concerning Section 7.1 of the Compact, the program under the Compact shall be implemented by complying with the Compact and in accordance with the domestic laws of Nepal.

11.   Concerning Section 8 of the Compact, Nepal declares that the electricity transmission project, all moveable and immovable assets, and land associated with the project shall be owned by the government of Nepal or entities of the Government of Nepal.

12.   Concerning the letter dated September 8, 2021 received by Nepal from the Millennium Challenge Corporation, the government understands that the responses in the said letter shall aid in the interpretation and implementation of the Compact.

Having the implementation of interpretative declaration, there is a provision in article 30 of the Vienna Convention of Laws of Treaties 1969.

Under the rule of interpretation, article 30 clearly says,

> "1. A treaty shall be interpreted in good faith ...to be given to the terms of the treaty ...in the light of its object and purpose. 2. The context for the interpretation of a treaty shall comprise...including its preamble and annexes: (a) any agreement ... was made between all the parties in connection

with the conclusion of the treaty; (b) any instrument … made by one or more parties … and accepted by the other parties as an instrument related to the treaty. 3. There shall be taken into account, together with the context: (a) any subsequent agreement between the parties regarding the interpretation of the treaty or the application of its provisions; (b) any subsequent practice in the application … agreement of the parties regarding its interpretation; (c) any relevant rules of international law applicable in the relations between the parties."

Several provisions of the interpretative declaration have been mentioned in the International Law Commission Report 2011. The 63rd General Assembly (April 26-June 3 and July 4-August 12, 2011) of the United Nations clearly states the definition of interpretative declaration and its formulation, determination, and condition and the difference between reservations and interpretative declarations, interpretative declarations regarding bilateral treaties and legal acceptance among others and their commentaries (UNGS, 2011).

Article 1.2 of the International Law Commission Report definition says, "Interpretative declaration" means a unilateral statement made by a State whereby that State purports to specify/clarify the meaning or scope of a treaty or certain of its provisions (United Nations, 2011). This means that any country can make an interpretive declaration when it ratifies the treaty.

The interpretative declaration is not binding but is also included in the Paris Agreement in linking with loss and damage. A vulnerable country like Nepal limits the effect of the Nepal Compact by making an interpretative declaration stating the acceptance of the Paris Agreement under general international law. Reservation does not permit in the Paris Agreement. Declaration simply states the declarant's opinion as to what the treaty means (LRI, Undated).

Interpretative declaration in connection with the signature of the UNFCCC (UN Framework Convention on Climate Change), Fiji stated, "The Government of Fiji declares its understanding that signature of the Convention shall, in no way, constitute a renunciation of any rights under international law concerning state responsibility for the adverse effects of climate change, and that no provisions in the Convention can be interpreted as derogating from the principles of general international law". Declarations were also made before ratification in Kiribati, Nauru, and Papua New Guinea (LRI, Undated).

For the very first time, Nepal has agreed to proclaim the interpretative declaration from the Parliament before the ratification of the MCC Agreement on February 27, 2022. The Nepal Compact shall be terminated if it violates Nepalese Law. The declaration saved the verge of a split of the ruling alliance.

Nepal's politics polarizes into right, left, and center wings. After the Oli-led government added a provision of MCC to be approved by the House in February 2019 which was not incorporated in the agreement in September 2017, there was an upheaval in the relations within and among the political parties. However, Oli Government did not table the Compact in the Secretariat in the Parliament. The rightist Nepali Congress was ambiguous to approve Nepal Compact. The then neither right nor left Oli-led government of the communist party tried hard to ratify Nepal Compact as it was, without amendment. But, the left-wing Prachanda and Madhav Kumar Nepal faction of the CPN criticized the PM Oli's stand and strongly demanded necessary amendments before the Compact's approval and was seeking national consensus. The mild-leftist Janata Samajbadhi Party and centrist Rashtriya Prajatantra Party also supported the Prachanda and Nepal factions. Small ultra-leftist parties were in a position to disprove the MCC stating as it was destined to encircle China or to make autonomous Tibet through illegal activities from Nepal. The voices of small ultra-right (culture-region-based) parties could not be heard.

But the world learned a lot having the poor status of Nepali politicians and their parties. It has been crystal clear that politics is similar to color-changing reptiles, i.e., the chameleon and the anole for Nepal. Rather than have perfection in the ideology, politics, foreign diplomacy, economy, and legal paradigms, each leader intends to have a self-benefit, then family, his faction/courtier, and the party. It has been rare for them to do politics focusing on people in general and the country and its sovereignty and non-alignment.

For example, the Nepali Congress was the main opposition party while the Oli-led two-thirds majority government. When the Oli government put forward the process of getting the Nepal Compact to be ratified by the parliament, NC leaders said that it should not be approved without amendment. When the Oli government collapsed due to controversy over the Nepal Compact, Deuba was appointed PM. Surprisingly the NC took U-turn. All the former pro-amendment leaders inserted pressure to approve Nepal Compact from the Parliament at any cost. But the role of the UML was confusing; neither had they voted in favor of nor against the motion. Besides, they were protesting against the speaker derailing the Parliamentary process of ratification of the Nepal Compact. Such a eunuch policy has been intensifying day by day since Nepal restored democracy in 1990.

The interpretive declaration is still not accepted by the MCC Headquarters. It would be a serious mistake for the US if it disobeyed the decision of the sovereign Parliament. Even if the US accepts it, there will have a positive attitude on the US among the people. Otherwise, the general perception is that the people have brought the MCC as the preparation for potential warfare to Cold War II. That ultimately creates tension between the US and China. The Cold War II shall be potential in such a case.

Freedom for formation of Fighting Ring

To strengthen developed countries themselves and their satellite sides, the superpowers are working hard to win people's minds through financial cooperation over the weak and poor countries by creating investment dramas. The rivalry between the US and the Soviet Union in Cold War I has now turned to escalate between the US and China in Cold War II. Sri Lanka has become a failed and bankrupted nation due to competition for financial cooperation or investment (Bloomberg, April 28, 2022, & Karunungan, April 7, 2022) from developed and muscled countries. China has established only one Belt and Road Initiative institution while the US has developed three institutions, namely Indo-Pacific Strategy, Build Back Better World, and Blue Dot Networks institutions. The question arises whether a fighting ring of geo-politics will be started from the ground of poor country Nepal. Their main goal is to protect themselves by increasing and tightening their fighting ring through heavily influence, control, and pressure in the name of financial assistance. These institutions have been a contentious issue for all in today's world.

Belt and Road Initiative

Since China's President Xi Jinping announced the launching of the BRI in 2013 and incorporated it in its Constitution in 2017 that intends to invest in connectivity on a transcontinental scale (The World Bank, March 29, 2019). BRI is a centerpiece of Chinese President Xi's foreign policy and diplomacy. In April 2019 at the second Belt and Road Forum gathering in Beijing Xi delivered his speech with proverbs, "The ceaseless inflow of rivers makes the ocean deep" (The Economist, June 4, 2020, and Westcott & Fang, April 27, 2019). As of March 2022, a total of 146 countries have signed to the BRI (Christoph, 2022). BRI is a "Silk Road Economic Belt" that was inspired by the notion of the Silk Road ancient trade routes network of China that had established during the Han Dynasty, some 2,000 years ago. The BRI is a 21st-century connectivity infrastructure investment initiative. It officially supports and connects the countries from Panama to Madagascar and South Africa to New Zealand (Kuo and Kommenda, July 30, 2018). This initiative is a bid to enhance regional connectivity for a brighter future (Xinhua, March 28, 2015). The BRI project has a target completion of 2049; which coincide with the centennial of the People's Republic of China's founding (CrowdReviews.com, March 25, 2019).

The G-7 countries have steadily highlighted the BRI's shortcomings in different international and academic forums concerning China's economic, political, military, and technological influence in the West (Skobalski, December 23, 2021). This is an ambitious flagship project that aims to join the community of collective destiny on the course to build a modern-day Silk Road through Asia (Giri, May 9, 2017). The BRI is also recognized as Digital Silk Road, namely WeChat and Alipay (Khatri, August 9, 2020).

There are arguments about whether the poor and developing countries will be led by a growing Chinese influence and control under the BRI. The world leaders of rich countries condemned the BRI projects as a Debt-Trap, economic imperialism, and neocolonialism. For instance, Sri Lanka is unable to repay money borrowed from Chinese banks and investments. As a result, Sri Lanka was forced to cough up the Hambantota port to China as it could not repay its past loans (Samaranayake, March 2, 2021). The influence and control may bring to mind memories of colonialism (Quintal, May 23, 2021). The Trump administration was the first to denounce China's global investment strategy. Accusing Chinese leader Xi Jinping of expanding his influence in developing countries, former Vice President Mike Pence said, "Today, that country is offering hundreds of billions of dollars in infrastructure loans to governments from Asia to Africa to Europe to even Latin America. Yet the terms of those loans are opaque at best, and the benefits flow overwhelmingly to Beijing" (Powell, November 4, 2021).

As far as rich-capitalist, guns for mass shooting, and war industries countries raise concerns having the implementation of the BRI, the poor and developing countries should carefully examine the proposed project(s) taking loans under the BRI. Nepal can also learn a lot from the present situation of its neighboring country Sri Lanka.

There is growing concern that Nepal is moving in the same direction as Sri Lanka. Remittances have declined. The price of diesel and petrol has not only gone up by 75 percent within a year but has also gone up in history. In the last six months (from October 2021 to March 2022), a total of Rs. 11 trillion Nepalese currency has been withdrawn from the banks. Many Nepalis have lost their jobs. Development and construction are stalled. The liquidity crisis in Nepal is continued from September 2021 and as of May 2022. Two-thirds of the Oli-led communist government had played a pivotal role in bringing about such a worse situation in the country. Many investors have lost their large sums of properties after the former commander of the Maoist Center and the current Finance Minister publicly said that he does not even know and needed to understand the problems of the Nepalese share market. If Finance Minister knew that the share market is a mirror of the country's economy, the huge investment of the people would not have so badly been sunk. In such a situation, Nepal is trying to get closer to the satellite-friendly country United States.

China supports aims at promoting Nepal's economic and social development, improving Nepal's living standards, fully respecting its national sovereignty and dignity, never interfering in Nepal's internal affairs, and not competing with any other country, or engaging in geopolitical games in Nepal (Yeping, April 14, 2022). China still doubts whether Nepal-China relationship transform into a comprehensive partnership integrating all projects under the BRI in the Himalayan valley.

Both countries reiterated their respect for each other's bilateral and national interests and their core concerns and agreed to accelerate the joint construction of the BRI gradually building a Trans-Himalayan Multi-dimensional Connectivity Network (an economic corridor between Nepal and China) to speed up the development of the both nations' cooperation. Pandey says, "Such ambitions are not unusual in Chinese strategic calculus — a similar approach could be noticed in China's interactions with other immediate neighbors such as Pakistan, Bangladesh, and Myanmar in particular (November 4, 2019).

BRI exceeds beyond hard infrastructure and economic development powers, even to the expansion of soft power and strategic plan to promote the Yuan as an international substitute to the US dollar. To achieve this, China will establish more multi-lateral infrastructure banks and economic firms as spider connectivity in Asia in particular and beyond which consequently weakens the influence of the existing USA-based organizations (Poudyal, 2019).

On March 15, 2019, the Nepali government endorsed the protocol of the Nepal-China Transit Transport Agreement (TTA) that ensures access to seven transit points in China – four seaports, namely Tianjin, Shenzhen, Lianyungang, and Zhanjiang, and three land ports, i.e., Lanzhou, Lhasa and Xigatse (Xinhua Silk Road Information Service, March 15, 2019). While the official visit of the then PM Oli to China in June 2018, both countries agreed to conduct a total of 14 different agreements including railway construction, the establishment of Mechanism for Facilitation on the Implementation of China-Nepal Cooperation Programs and Projects in Nepal, among others (THT Online, June 21, 2018).

In a joint communiqué issued after the two-day (October 12 and 13, 2019) state visit of Chinese President Xi Jinping, Nepal and China announced that they would develop their everlasting friendship as a strategic partnership for development and prosperity. Among the 14-point statement, number one highlights the BRI as an important opportunity to deepen mutual and beneficial cooperation to maintain peace, stability, and development in this South Asia region. Declaring the bilateral relationship between Nepal and China has entered into a new phase, the communiqué said, "Both sides decided to, based on the Five Principles of Peaceful Coexistence, Charter of the United Nations and principles of good neighborliness, elevate Nepal-China Comprehensive Partnership of Cooperation Featuring Ever-lasting Friendship to Strategic Partnership of Cooperation" (Ministry of Foreign Affairs Nepal, October 13, 2019). President Xi returned to Beijing after a tumultuous round of meetings with Nepali leaders and others. Nepal reiterated its firm commitment to a 'one-China policy' and 'Taiwan is an inalienable part of Chinese territory, and 'Tibet affairs are China's internal affairs. Nepal does not allow any anti-China activities on its soil (Giri, October 14, 2019).

It is to be noted that there was the first time a joint statement issued by Nepal and China mentioned having the forthcoming strategic partnership. For two and a half years since the joint communiqué was released, no one knows how the strategic partnership for development and prosperity will move forward. On the one hand, neither any modality has been made nor has Nepal paid attention to it. On the other side, strategic partnership is a vague phrase itself. The strategic partnership is to be strengthened and developed the country and set up the developmental agenda.

Nepal had officially chosen 35 projects on the connectivity and energy components under the BRI projects but has been trimmed down to nine. Among the nine projects identified are three road projects, two hydroelectricity projects, one cross-border railway, one cross-border transmission line, and one technical institution under the name of the late Madan Bhandari. They are named as Upgradation of Rasuwagadhi-Kathmandu road, Kimathanka-Hile road construction, Dipayal to the south border with China, Tokha-Bidur road, Galchhi-Rasuwagadhi-Kerung 400kv transmission line, Keyrung-Kathmandu rail (feasibility study), Tamor hydroelectricity project, and Phuket Karnali Hydro Electric Project (Giri, January 18, 2019)

Everyone agrees that Nepal should take maximum benefit from China's economic development through the BRI framework. While Nepal asks for grants, China says that those projects under the BRI are largely loan-based. But, there is a question of whether Nepal will be able to pay back those loans while Pakistan and Sri Lanka face debt problems with China. Some scholars described the BRI projects as a debt trap (Bhattarai, June 2, 2019) diplomacy.

On April 12, 2022, while a debt trap was crisis-ridden, Sri Lanka's central bank governor P Nandalal Weerasinghe announced, "It has come to a point that making debt payments are challenging and impossible. The best action that can be taken is to restructure debt and avoid a hard default (Srinivasan, April 12, 2022). It means the Sri Lanka Government temporarily suspended the payment of its foreign debts (ANI, April 12, 2022). Pakistan may also be in a difficult situation to repay the debt loan. China Pakistan Economic Corridor is a $50 billion flagship BRI component that is invested in power plants, industrial clusters, road, and rail upgrades. About half the money pledged by China has already been invested (Aamir, November 30, 2022).

The BRI and other investments across Nepal face significant resistance from the local population as many believe that the Chinese lucrative promises of infrastructure development will harm the Himalayan Kingdom. African countries have cancelled their development contracts for Chinese projects on which Nepal needs to take another look at the BRI as a debt trap (Kumar, October 2, 2021). Quoting Prachanda saying Thapa writes, "Nepal firmly adheres to the One China policy not only verbally, but also in action, and will not allow any external forces to engage in anti-China activities in Nepal (September 12, 2019). Out of 195 countries, 146 of them have signed up for the infrastructure and ambitious BRI projects across the world. One of the countries signed up to the BRI is Nepal which is itself caught in a geopolitical tug-of-war between Beijing and Washington (Ghlionn, February 28, 2022).

India objects BRI not because BRI is strategic geopolitical, but for its enmity with Pakistan. Western countries have been protesting against the BRI since its inception, which continues to this day. However, due to the US pressure and influence, China's BRI projects neither have been selected nor have there been public discussions like the MCC in Nepal.

Indo-pacific strategy

The US is an Indo-Pacific Strategic power holder, which in short form widely called IPS. The IPS ranges from western coast of the Indian Ocean to west coast of the US, home to more than half of the world's people that occupies nearly two-thirds of the world's economy. About half of the US military is based in the region than in any other outside the United States (Biden, September 24, 2021). US President Joe Biden said, "We envision an Indo-Pacific that is open, connected, prosperous, resilient, and secure..." (September 24, 2021) for generations to come. This paper was submitted at Quad Leaders' Summit in Washington on September 24, 2021. The initiative focuses on three areas, namely economics, governance, and security (Hartman, September 23, 2019).

The objective of the security is to maintain peace and stability across the Taiwan Strait. Having the coverage, the paper states, "We will focus on every corner of the region from Northeast Asia and Southeast Asia, to South Asia and Oceania, including the Pacific islands" (Indo-Pacific Strategy of the United States of America, February 2022). Many European countries demonstrated a keen interest in playing a greater role in the Indian and Pacific Oceans and vowed to strengthen between EU and Indo-Pacific countries further (Rajagopalan, February 25, 2022).

On March 19, 2022, addressing the International Forum on Security and Strategy launched by the Centre for

International Security and Strategy of Tsinghua University, China's Vice Foreign Minister Le Yucheng stated that the US' Indo-Pacific strategy is as dangerous as NATO's eastward expansion in Europe that resulted in Russia's military offensive against Ukraine (NDTV, March 20, 2022).

The Department of Defense has shared values that support promoting long-term peace and prosperity for all in the Indo-Pacific. It accepts policies or actions that threaten or undermine the rules-based international order: an order that benefits all nations (June 1, 2019). The Defense Report stated that the shared strategic vision is uninterrupted despite an increasingly complex security environment. Inter-state strategic competition is the primary concern for US national security. The report says, "In particular, the People's Republic of China…seeks to reorder the region to its advantage by leveraging military modernization, influence operations, and predatory economics to coerce other nations (June 1, 2019). The region includes the world's largest economies: the United States, China, and Japan, and six of the world's fastest growing economies, namely India, Cambodia, Laos, Burma, Nepal, and the Philippines" (June 1, 2019).

The US Defense aim is to extend its major partnership with India and other developing countries. On June 8, 2016, the joint statement of US-India acknowledged that India is a Major Defense Partner of the US (Gould, June 8, 2016). The Indo-Pacific Strategy Report says, "The United States seeks to expand our defense relationship with Nepal, focused on HA/DR, peacekeeping operations, defense professionalization, ground force capacity, and counter-terrorism" (Ghimire, June 1, 2019, & Department of State. (2017, November 4). The Chinese-affiliated/satellite powers understand that IPS is meant to weaken encircling China from strategic important Nepal. That is why the communist bloc led by China firmly believes, that the US seeks to build an Indo-Pacific version of NATO (Bloomberg News, March 8, 2022) in this continent. Many have understood that the MCC is an important initiative under the Indo-Pacific Strategy.

Build Back Better World

The Group of Seven (G7) richest democratic countries sought to counter China's growing economic influence on developing countries establishing a Build Back Better World (B3W). The B3W is designed to rebuild grand infrastructures in developing nations that could rival President Xi Jinping of China's multi-trillion-dollar BRI (Steve & Faulconbridge, June 13, 2021, and South China Morning Post, June 12, 2021) which is launched in June 2021. Led by the US Government, the G7 leaders have a plan to provide a values-driven, high-standard, and transparent infrastructure partnership on the course to fulfill low- and middle-income countries' infrastructure demands. It helps narrow the $40 trillion needed by developing nations by 2035 (The White House, June 12, 2021). It coordinates in mobilizing the private-sector in the areas focusing on climate, health, security, digital technology, and gender equity. The finance institutions include the Development Finance Corporation, USAID, EXIM, the Millennium Challenge Corporation, the US Trade and Development Agency, and the Transaction Advisory Fund (The White House, June 12, 2021). The global financial institution aims to build a global network to build roads, bridges, airports, power plants, and ports. The objective of the global infrastructure building program is to promote economic development and inter-regional connectivity.

The US and G7 intended to endorse the guiding principles for the B3W which comprise good governance, climate change, strong strategic partnerships, mobilizing private capital through development finance, and enhancing the impact of multilateral public finance. The US, Canada, Britain, Germany, Italy, France, and Japan aim that the B3W plan offers an alternative to China's growing BRI clout (South China Morning Post, June 12, 2021). Biden highlights that China is not a democratic country that practices predatory lending or debt-trap diplomacy in OBOR (rfa, June 23, 2021).

Money and clear vision are the sole mechanisms for the course of the development any country. If the development of the country is envisaged only by the multiparty democracy, that is only a partial truth.

Blue Dot Network

The BDN (Blue Dot Network) is a mechanism that certifies infrastructure projects which are to meet international quality criteria and standards. The network is a multi-stakeholder initiative which is launched by the United States, Japan, and Australia to promote principles of sustainable infrastructure development around the world. It aims to promote globally recognized market-driven, transparent, Paris Agreement-aligned, and financially, socially, and environmentally sustainable infrastructure projects (www.state.gov/blue-dot-network/ & Herman, January 31, 2020). It was jointly established in November 2019 on the sidelines of the 35th ASEAN Summit at the Indo-Pacific Business Forum (Kuo, April 7, 2020) in Thailand with access to $60 billion of capital. It was initially led by the US International Development Finance

Corporation, Japan Bank for International Cooperation, and the Department of Foreign Affairs and Trade of Australia (Explained Desk, February 26, 2020). The notion of the BDN is to bring together the Government, private sector, and civil society of the world, but its function is shadowed either by IPS or BRI and B3W. On June 7, 2021, the OECD commits to supporting the BDN at a meeting of the Executive Consultation Group in Paris, France (Cormann, June 7, 2021). On June 12, 2021, the G7 announced the adoption of the B3W initiative built off the progress and principles of the Blue Dot Network to counter the BRI (rfa, June 23, 2021)

Two big powers, namely the USA and China intensify their arguments and engagement with growing deep infrastructure development, political, and ideological interests in Nepal too. While Nepal signed a Memorandum of Understanding (MoU) on bilateral cooperation under the framework of the BRI or B & R on May 12, 2017 (Ying, May 12, 2017), as a rising economical reconfiguration in the World's development (Shrestha, December 2, 2021), the US Nepal Compact was also signed by Nepal four months and two days later.

To further expand trade and technology, China moves forward to invest billions of US dollars in infrastructure projects, namely railways, power grids, and ports across Asia, Africa, and East Europe. Besides, it has a desire to strengthen a greater leadership role in global affairs by its rising power and status (Smith, February 16, 2021). On contrary, the United States and its allied Western nations not only increase their pressure and influence in the Indo-Pacific region but moreover to secede Tibet.

This means that Western countries are investing full economic power and security measures to counter the impact of BRI by establishing various development organizations. Their unhealthy competition from small, landlocked, and poor countries like Nepal will have to face not only the potential for Cold War II but also to encounter warfare.

Freedom for Arguments

Before MCC formation, US President George W. Bush called for a set of clear and concrete objectives to fund the nations that have open markets and sustainable budget policies. As per Bush's announcement, the architects of MCC at the National Security Council codified it in the 2002 National Security Strategy stating, "[T]he Millennium Challenge Account will reward countries that have demonstrated real policy change and challenge those that have not implemented reform" (Parks, April 1, 2019). Analyzing data from 14,000 observations and 118 response countries, the author says "38 percent of the low- and lower-middle-income countries that could have plausibly been influenced by the MCC eligibility criteria—between 2004 and 2010" (Parks, April 1, 2019).

The MCC was created by the US Congress in early 2004 (Hewko, 2010) as an independent US foreign aid agency that is helping to fight against global poverty. It focuses on the grant to the country that has good policies, ownership, and results. The MCC clearly says, "These investments not only support stability and prosperity in partner countries but also enhance American interests" (www.mcc.gov/about). It further states, "MCC is a good investment for the American people" (www.mcc.gov/about). It invests in three primary categories: first, the Compacts which provide large, five-year grants for selected countries that meet MCC's eligibility criteria; second the Concurrent compacts for regional investments grant to promote cross-border economic integration and regional trade collaboration; and lastly, the threshold programs that provide smaller grants focusing to a firm commitment to improving their policy performance (www.mcc.gov/about).

The MCC is one of the dazzling innovations of the eight-year rule of the Bush Presidency (Rieffel & Fox, 2008). The MCC approved 22 compacts starting from 2005 to 2010. They are Madagascar (2005), Honduras (2005), Cape Verde (2005), Nicaragua (2005), Georgia (2005), Benin (2006), Vanuatu (2006), Armenia (2006), Ghana (2006), Mali (2006), El Salvador (2006), Mozambique (2007), Lesotho (2007), Morocco (2007), Mongolia (2007), Tanzania (2007), Burkina Faso (2008), Namibia (2008), Senegal (2009), Moldova (2009), Philippines (2010), and Jordan (2010) (Tarnoff, November 16, 2010).

By the end of March 2022, the MCC expanded its works in a total of 51 countries either in compact or threshold programs. Of these, more than half (51 percent) including Côte d'Ivoire, Ghana, Ethiopia, Kenya, Liberia, Morocco, Namibia, and Rwanda are in Africa. Of the 81 programs operated/operating, more than two-thirds of 33 (41%) projects lie under the threshold programs in Albania, Ethiopia, Guatemala, Honduras, Indonesia, Jordon, Kenya, Kosovo, Liberia, Peru, Philippines, Rwanda, Sierra Leon, Ukraine, Uganda, Zambia, and among others (www.mcc.gov/where-we-work). Compacts belong to 47 (58%) projects in 35 countries including Armenia, Cote d'Ivoire, El Salvador, Georgia, Ghana, Honduras, Indonesia, Jordon, Kosovo, Madagascar, Mozambique, Namibia, Nicaragua, Philippines, Senegal, Sierra Leone, Sri Lanka, Tanzania, and Tunisia unlike only one project under the Concurrent Compacts for Regional Investments. Among 81 projects, 35 have already been completed; 12 are under the proposed or development phase, and 10 are implementing phase (www.mcc.gov/where-we-work).

Of the 51, 22 (43%) countries have implemented more than one compact or threshold or both projects in nearly two-decade of MCC's establishment on the course of reducing poverty through growth. Two compacts and one threshold program have been launched in Zambia, Tanzania, Malawi, Indonesia, and Burkina Faso countries (www.mcc.gov/where-we-work). One compact and one threshold program are carried out in each Timor Leste, Sierra Leone, Philippines, Paraguay, Niger, Mozambique, Moldova, Liberia, Kosovo, Jordon, and Honduras countries. Each Morocco, Lesotho, Ghana, El Salvador, and Cabo Verda countries have been conducted two compacts programs (www.mcc.gov/where-we-work) by the MCC, whereas Kenya in December 2019 has received a single threshold program (www.mcc.gov/where-we-work/program/kenya-proposed-threshold-program).

Sri Lanka in December 2020 (Dahal, April 21, 2021) and Ethiopia in December 2021 (www.mcc.gov/where-we-work/program/ethiopia-proposed-threshold-program) discontinued the MCC Compact. On March 28, 2016, the MCC Board voted to suspend the compact's partnership with Tanzania (www.mcc.gov/where-we-work/program/tanzania-proposed-compact).

A total of 12 countries, namely Belize, Indonesia, Kenya, Kiribati, Kosovo, Lesotho, Malawi, Mozambique, Sierra Leone, Timor-Leste, Tunisia, and Zambia are in the state project development phase. The projects of the 12 countries are in the implementation phases which are Benin, Cote d'Ivoire, Ghana, Kosovo, Mongolia, Morocco, Niger, Senegal, The Gambia, and Togo (www.mcc.gov/where-we-work).

Out of 12 threshold programs, only two Tanzania and Burkina Faso have proceeded to compact programs. Two, the Philippines and Timor Leste are working on the compact proposals (mcc.gov). The Solomon Islands signed the MCC in January 2022 whereas Nepal ratified the Compact on February 27, 2022 (MCC, January 2022).

On September 3, 2021, Nepal sent 11-point contentious issues or objectionable questions about the agreement to the MCC headquarters in Washington (Pandey, September 4, 2021). In response to those contentious questions in five days or on September 8 (MCC, September 8, 2021), the MCC officials tried to provide clarifications to all 11 major questions and supplementary trepidations raised by the Government of Nepal (Ministry of Finance) (Shrestha & Giri, September 8, 2021, and Nepal Live Today, September 8, 2021).

At the request of the Government of Nepal, the US Government started working with Nepal in 2012 through the development of an MCC compact. During the past years, each new Government and political party in Nepal, when in power, expressed to conclude an MCC Compact for economic development in Nepal. The MCC is focused on economic development by helping to build electricity lines and improve roads. The US Government reaffirmed that there is no military component and US law prohibits it on the MCC (https://np.usembassy.gov/mcc-in-nepal-top-ten-facts/). Nepal does not need to "join" or "sign up" for anything to participate in having the attainment of the MCC. The $500 million is purely a grant, with no string of pearls attached which means no hidden clauses. Nepalis proposed and decided on projects that will fund based on Nepal's priorities. And MCC's model requires hiring Nepalis to lead the implementation of the projects. MCC project tenders are open, transparent, and available to everyone. In every country where MCC works, parliamentary ratification is required to understand the project   (https://np.usembassy.gov/mcc-in-nepal-top-ten-facts/).

Responding to the letter of Finance Minister Janardan Sharma, Fatima Sumar, a mid-level staff of the MCC replied to the contentious questions. Some of the important Nepal questions and MCC's answers have mentioned below:

Question 1: What is the basis that the support under MCC is selfless?

Answer: The purpose of MCC is to reduce poverty through economic growth. It has a goal to rapidly improve the lives of the Nepalese people. Nepal Compact is a grant for Nepal to complete the electricity transmission and road maintenance projects. These projects shall be completed within the five-year timeline.

Question 2: What is the basis for claiming that Nepal is not prioritized under a military strategy?

Answer: US Government prohibits the MCC from using grant funds for any military purpose. There is no link between the Nepal Compact and any military alliance or defense strategy. For the eligibility for the grant, a country must: (1) be classified as a low income or lower middle-income country classified by the World Bank, and (2) pass the annual MCC country scorecard that focuses on the country's commitment to just and democratic governance, investing in people and economic freedom.

Question 3: Was the MCC agreement concluded in line with Nepal's own needs and demands?

Answer: The Nepal Compact projects were selected by the Government of Nepal in consultation with private sectors and civil society. Nepal has designed the electricity transmission project as a project of national pride.

Question 4: The MCC agreement has been classified as an international agreement in an attempt to weaken the Constitution and laws of Nepal. What ground is there, as per article 7.1 of the agreement, to claim that it is not so?

Answer: The status of an international agreement means that the implementation of compact projects will proceed following the laws of Nepal except in the rare instance. Nepal Compact projects will be implemented according to the mutually agreed upon terms of the compact and the Constitution of Nepal. The Law Ministry reviewed all terms of the MCC Nepal Compact, including article 7.1, and concluded that the compact provisions do not conflict with the laws of Nepal.

Question 5: Many development projects in Nepal do not necessarily seek parliamentary approval. Why is Nepal Compact necessary to ratify the agreement alone?

Answer: During compact development, the MCC asks each partner government what their country's domestic law requires for the compact to have the status of an international agreement which requires avoiding any specific conflicts in the future.

Question 6: After parliamentary ratification of the agreement, why is parliamentary approval not required for the agreement's parts, the implementation agreement, or amendments to the project? Is it not due to the strategic location of Nepal in global politics and conflict and the intention to use that strategic location?

Answer: The MCC Nepal Compact, which has already been signed, cannot be amended now. The MCC Nepal Compact was signed in September 2017 following extensive discussions between MCC and the Government of Nepal, including Nepal's Ministry of Law, Justice, and Parliamentary Affairs. But Compact Section 6.2(b) allows for modification. Section 6.2(c) specifically provides such modifications are not 'amendments' and do not need parliamentary ratification.

Question 7: Is MCC under the Indo-Pacific Strategy?

Answer: No, MCC Nepal is not an agreement under the IPS. MCC is the agreement between the MCC and Nepal government.

Question 8: Is Nepal a member of IPS or can it become a member of it?

Answer: MCC Nepal is not an agreement under the IPS. Any decision of Nepal on the IPS is separate and independent from the MCC.

Question 9: How is it possible for MCC to be put under IPS as IPS was formed in 2017?

Answer: MCC was established in 2004 with a singular focus on poverty reduction through economic growth. The MCC is neither an agreement under the IPS, nor is it a part of US military strategy.

Question 10: Why has the implementation agreement signed between Finance Minister Yubaraj Khatiwada and MCC Vice President Anthony Welcher on September 29, 2019, not been made public yet?

Answer: The Program Implementation Agreement, signed on September 29, 2019, has been publicly available since signing, including on the MCA-Nepal website (www.mcanp.org).

Question 11: There are controversial Articles such as 2.8, 3.1(f), 3.7, 3.8, and 5.3(a), among others in the Nepal Compact. How should they be clarified?

Answer: As per Article 2.8, the MCC wanted to exempt the project staff from receiving an international level of remuneration and benefits, from all kinds of taxes. Having the provision of Article 3.1(f) stated that the project will be implemented with a 26 percent contribution from Nepal but the intellectual property will fully belong to the MCC, but it replied all intellectual property belongs to Nepal ignoring the previous stands. Nepal Government will use its best efforts to maintain all records and documents on Article 3.7 of the agreement which previously stated that all the original records of the project need to be submitted to the MCC. The Auditor General of Nepal shall conduct the audit of the Compact project despite the earlier provision of the audit that will be conducted by the US-based certified accounting firm as per Article 3.8. Article 5.1(a) has a provision that MCC may terminate the funding by giving 30 days prior written notice to the Government of Nepal, but both Compact and Nepal have the individual ability to terminate the compact with 30 days' notice.

The Government of India should support the infrastructure project to be constructed within Nepal (Annex-5a) and condition on Electronic Regulation Commission Act (Annex 5b). In additional conditions precedent to entry into force says, "The Government must have submitted a plan, in form and substance acceptable to MCC, and consented to by the governments of India, memorializing (i) key financial and technical terms for the construction of the New Butwal-Gorakhpur cross-border transmission line, and (ii) operational principles for the New Butwal-Gorakhpur cross-border transmission line".

The disputes over the Nepal Compact much intensified while David J Ranz, Acting Assistant Secretary for South Asia at the US State Department on May 14, 2019, said, "Millennium Challenge Corporation Compact program was one of the most important initiatives being implemented in

Nepal under the US Indo-Pacific Strategy" (Nepal, May 15, 2019). He further argued, "Regional connectivity is another critical aspect of our goals in the Indo-Pacific Strategy." In an interaction with a select group of journalists, Ranz said a whole-of-government effort was underway to expand US engagement with the Indo-Pacific region, including Nepal, to ensure it is free, open, and operates on a rules-based system (Nepal, May 15, 2019).

The IPS Report 2019 describes China as a strategic competitor and revisionist power. Under the leadership of the US, Japan, France, India, Australia, and New Zealand emphasize rules-based order through high-level statements in 2018. In this Indian Ocean Region, the US specifically replies on five strategic partners: India, Sri Lanka, Bangladesh, the Maldives, and Nepal (Ankit, June 11, 2029) to share regional security challenges. The US firmly believes on Indo-Pacific is the most consequential region for America's future. The US military brass added that the US works with countries in the region on military training and maritime security. Ankit Panda says, "The United States expects our allies and partners to shoulder a fair share of the burden of responsibility to protect against common threats" (Ankit, June 11, 2029). Thus, Shrestha says, "The MCC has since been redefined to suit America's military design in what they now call Indo-Pacific region targeting China" (Shrestha, February 16, 2022). There has been a clear message that a Common threat would happen in China. Pointing out the MCC Shrestha writes, "Nepal's participation in its present form will require us to act "against common threats" that would be our valuable neighbor, China" (Shrestha, February 16, 2022).

The US wants to share the burden of the National Security Strategy to pursue cooperation and reciprocity among its satellite allies, partners, and aspiring partners. When the US pools resources and shares responsibility for its common defense believing that its security burden converts lighter and more cost-effective. The US-led IPS has already strengthened its alliances with Japan, Australia, South Korea, Thailand, and the Philippines. The 2019 IPS Report on page 21 says,

> "These alliances are indispensable to peace and security in the region and our investments in them will continue to pay dividends for the United States and the world, far into the future. We have also taken steps to expand partnerships with Singapore, Taiwan, New Zealand, and Mongolia. Within South Asia, we are working to operationalize our Major Defense Partnership with India, while pursuing emerging partnerships with Sri Lanka, the Maldives, Bangladesh, and Nepal. We are also continuing to strengthen security relationships with partners in Southeast Asia, including Vietnam, Indonesia, and Malaysia, and sustaining engagements with Brunei, Laos, and Cambodia. In the Pacific Islands, we are enhancing our engagement to preserve a free and open Indo-Pacific, maintain access, and promote our status as a security partner of choice" (Department of Defense, June 1, 2019).

Ranz further said that Indo-Pacific efforts were focused on three areas: economics, security, and governance. The US has been launching several new programs and initiatives under these themes. Ranz made it clear that the IPS is not an alliance or agreement. It was about freedom, freedom of navigation, freedom of the press, protection of the sovereignty of countries of the region, enabling them to make the best decisions for the people of those countries both politically and economically free of any kind of coercion (Nepal, May 15, 2019).

Criticizing the own party CPN Oli-led Government as Nepal being a battleground of foreign actors, Chief Whip Dev Gurung said, "The Americans are coming every month to Kathmandu and saying that Nepal is very much a part of the Indo-Pacific Strategy. The foreign ministry should take firm action and stand against the Indo-Pacific Strategy" (Giri, June 19, 2019).

The then Finance Minister Yubaraj Khatiwada registered the Nepal Compact at the Federal Parliament for its ratification in July 2019. However, he did not dare to table before the House for approval owing to massive disputes within and beyond parties. The former Nepal Communist Party, including its Chief Whip Dev Gurung and Speaker Krishna Bahadur Mahara, did not put its priority on ratification. Even though, on October 19, 2020, incumbent PM Oli allegedly blamed Mahara for delaying the ratification process.

The provision of India's approval is necessary for the implementation of the Nepal Compact made huge disputes between those who wanted to ratify without any revision at any cost and a large section of the people opposed it. But, the favoring force argues that India's approval requires only the cross-border Butwal-Gorakhpur transmission line that facilitates the import/export of electricity to and from Nepal. The communists and the people often chanted anti-India slogans and protested it as a symbol of nationalism, neither like the word Indo nor India. India itself is also a responsibility for bringing about such a situation. There has been a clear history that India always tends to form an unstable government in Nepal on the course to control

Nepal's natural resources and Nepalese lands through the porous border in the name of human insecurity.

On the other, Washington pursued, "Nepal's central role in free and open Indo-Pacific" while the then Foreign Minister Pradeep Gyawali's visit to the United States in December 2018" (Giri, May 15, 2019). There were dissenting leaders within and outside the ruling party and civil society who demanded to amend some of the suspicious provisions of the MCC before its ratification.

The CPN and other small revolutionary fringe communists expressed their objections to a clause concerning the ratification of the agreement by the House of Representatives. Leaders objected to the House's approval as an offensive clause. They used to argue that the MCC is a part of the Indo-Pacific Strategy. This is often advocated by Dr. Bhim Rawal, the senior CPN-UML leader including many others. There are controversial points in the agreements which are quite contentious that implicate seriously on Nepal's sovereignty, economy, foreign policy, security, and diplomacy (Chand, August 2021).

Even after the endorsement of the MCC on February 27, 2022, the fierce opponent of the MCC Nepal Compact Bhim Rawal said that the MCC compact was endorsed in haste and amid protests. The PM Deuba and other top leaders were not sensitive about the national interest. Article 279 of the Constitution stipulates that any agreement needs the backing of a two-thirds majority, but the MCC was passed by a simple majority. The several provisions of the MCC go against the national interests. If such provisions are implemented, the domestic laws, the right to self-determination, and national independence will be compromised (Karn, March 18, 2022). Rawal was sharply criticized before the endorsement of the MCC. He pointed out that the MCC will be passed by parliament without amendment; it would turn the country into a conflict of power (People's Review, December 26, 2021). Former PM Jhalanath Khanal, the three-member led Task Force by the ruling party to study the MCC warns stating that it will be disastrous if Government Passes MCC (Republica, February 25, 2022). All professionals of Nepal from politicians to bureaucrats, technicians, social stalwarts, teachers and students, religious to political cadres, and others were protested, argued, and criticized the US-established MCC.

There are several examples of fully and partially terminating compacts for numerous reasons. In April 2005, Madagascar became the first country to receive an MCC compact but terminated in August 2009 (Press Release May 20, 2010) due to undemocratic power transfer. Nicaragua compact was partially terminated in June 2009 (Report No. M-000-12-003-S, March 30, 2011) and the Honduras compact was in September 2009 (MCC, May 7, 2020). The compact was terminated from Mali following a military coup in May 2012 (Fishbein & Haile, 2012). Above mentioned causes may also repeat in Nepal in the operation of the MCC.

All international treaties signed by the Government of Nepal overcome domestic law in case of conflict as per the Nepal Treaty Act 1990. The Act clearly states, "In case of the provisions of a treaty, to which Nepal or Government of

Nepal is a party upon its ratification accession, acceptance, or approval by the Parliament, inconsistent with the provisions of prevailing laws, the inconsistent provision of the law shall be void for that treaty, and the provisions of the treaty shall be enforceable as good as Nepalese laws". But the MCC Nepal compact is an agreement, not a treaty. All Nepalis have only one question, why is the MCC agreement to be ratified by the Federal Parliament recognizing it as a bi-or-multilateral treaty? No concrete answer is received yet by the concerned official of the MCC, Washington.

On the other hand, Nepal never maintains protocol status in regards to the MCC process for agreement and endorsement for the Central Parliament. The chief example is that the PM Deuba and Prachanda sent a joint letter to the MCC secretarial level official asking sometimes for its endorsement. This is just a small example of how far we have fallen behind the money and muscle of the US. People in general firmly believe that the MCC is a politico-economic part of the IPS warfare for the geostrategic country Nepal. The almost two-thirds majority holding the Oli-led Government and Communist Party of Nepal was ousted from the Government in three-and-half years and the party split into three-section because of the contentious issue of the MCC.

Whether someone protests or not, the MCC plan is sure to leave a lasting significant impact in Nepal. The prime effect of the MCC shall potential for Cold War II for the observation of both China and India. Nepal has porous cross-border facilities for both countries. 'Watch to India' and 'encircle to China' using Nepalese land, (proxy) leaders, and bureaucrats shall be the core clandestine objective of the MCC Nepal Compact. The formation of a new government under the leadership of Deuba has been the lottery to introduce vested interest of the US foreign and strategic policy but a major setback to China. The US-India friendly relations may turn warfare on the issue to see Nepal in future. India is agreed to encircle China and make China weak, but compete with the US because of US policy to watch India too using Nepalese land. Such conflict may further advance the potentiality of Cold War II where Nepal may victimize further.

Freedom of China's Scary

Even after the ratification of the MCC by the House, it could not be escaped from controversies. There were lots of protests and arguments being continued on the suspicions that where the MCC linked with the US-led IPS and a few other provisions included in the agreement that will overcome Nepal's laws in case of conflict while operating in Nepal. Such controversies have given space for neighborhoods to talk about the MCC and its surrounding suspiciousness. China is at the forefront of arguments or comments on the Nepal Compact. The first reason for China's reaction was that a large section of the communist party leaders strongly stood against ratification of the compact, disagreeing that the MCC is part of IPS which aims to counter China (Ghimire, January 9, 2020). On June 9, 2022, the Commanding General of the United States Army Pacific Charles Flynn arrived for a four-day visit in Nepal.

The Nepal Compact's irritating shadow and critical question are why did the grant of a substantially small size comparative to Nepal's economy have to face such a rigid resistance? The answer is, unlike the historical silence diplomacy since long been adopted, China directly meddles in Nepal's decision-making process to strategically push the US to the sidelines in the regional geopolitical domain (Wagle, February 28, 2022). In China's view, the MCC is not only related to Nepal's internal politics but also to regional geopolitics. On the other, while NATO was being encircled by Russia expanding its memberships and Russia invaded war into Ukraine, the conscious Nepali doubted whether the same strategic-tactical process would be pursued in Nepal too.

Having the Nepal Compact ratification along with Interpretive Declaration, Chinese Foreign Ministry Spokesman Wang Wenbin said, "We noted the decision and the declaration by the Nepalese parliament" (Varma, February 28, 2022). China always supports Nepal's selection of an independent path of development and its internal affairs. Wang further that China repeatedly stressed that international formal cooperation should follow the principle of mutual interest, equal treatment, and fully respecting the sovereignty of the country and the will of its people. It should not interfere in other countries' internal affairs by engaging in coercive diplomacy, undermining the sovereignty and interest of the people (Varma, February 28, 2022).

On March 26, 2022, State Councilor and Chinese Foreign Minister Wang Yi held official talks to Nepal with his counterpart Nepali Foreign Minister Narayan Khadka in Kathmandu. Wang put forward three types of assistance to Nepal. They are to follow a development trajectory that suits Nepal's conditions; pursue a sovereign domestic and foreign policy; and further profoundly participate in the construction path of the BRI (Ministry of Foreign Affairs, March 27, 2022).

On March 7, 2022, China daily's editorial writes, "No matter how the Nepalese see it, the US has its agenda and its geopolitical objectives. And the consequences may be serious should any part of the compact be used against neighboring China" (New Spotlight Online, May 7, 2022).

On February 24, 2022, or three-day prior to the Nepal Compact ratification, Song Tao, a senior politician currently serving as the Head of the International Liaison Department of the Communist Party of China held zoom talks with CPN (UML) and CPN (US). Those leaders discussed the implementation of the agreements reached between Nepal and China, strengthening the mutual understanding among the parties, and other cooperation in various fields (Pandey, February 24, 2022). The talks left a significant impact on economic diplomacy. Why the Nepal-China projects have been kept in shadow while there had been so many talks having the ratification of the MCC. The talks gave immense psychological pressure not to ratify the MCC also.

Hua Chunying, who is the Chinese Assistant Minister of Foreign Affairs as well as Foreign Ministry Spokesperson and Director General, Information Department, People's Republic of China, concluded that MCC was a form of coercive diplomacy the US was pursuing in Nepal (Khabarhub, February 23, 2022). During a regular press briefing in Beijing, previously on February 18, Chunying said, "If the US is giving a gift to Nepal, then why is it setting a deadline. It should not interfere in other countries internal affairs, attach political strings, or engage in coercive diplomacy, still less undermining other countries' sovereignty and interests out of one's self-interests (Global Times, February 23, 2022). Chunying further asked, "Is it a gift or Pandora's box? I'm afraid it will turn out like a Nepali saying: It looks good, but you will find the meat difficult to chew" (Himalayan News Service, February 24, 2022)

Hou Yanqi (Hou), Chinese Ambassador to Nepal stated that Nepal should become a common garden for all friendly nations, not a fighting ring for geopolitical games. She further elaborates, "Nepal is China's good neighbor and good friend. The two countries have always respected each other's sovereignty and territorial integrity, not interfering in each other's internal affairs, while watching over each other and sharing a common destiny, setting a model for countries big, and small to treat each other as equals and to cooperate for win-win results" (Yeping, April 14, 2022). Nepal should accept any economic support and there is no harm to the country in endorsing the MCC. China stated that the ratification of the MCC has noted along with the interpretive declaration.

Under Secretary for Civilian Security, Democracy, and Human Rights and US Special Coordinator for Tibetan Issues, Uzra Zeya traveled May 20–22 to Nepal in the name of deep cooperation on human rights and democratic governance goals, and to advance humanitarian priorities (US Department of State, May 16, 2022).

Commenting on Zeya's visit to Nepal, Anil Giri states that Beijing seems to be wary of a series of visits from the US and a senior official's recent meetings with Tibetan refugees in Kathmandu. During the 14th meeting of the Nepal-China Bilateral Consultative Mechanism at the end of May 2022, the Chinese side expressed their reservations over US Uzra Zeya's visits to the Tibetan refugees' camp in Nepal (May 26, 2022).

Commenting on Zeya's visit to Nepal and Tibetan refugees camps Professor Hu Shisheng, a Senior Research Fellow and the Director of the Institute for South Asian Studies at the China Institutes of Contemporary International Relations (CICIR) states that if the Sino-US tension and Sino-Indian conflict escalate in the coming days, Nepal will have to face more pressure from the US and India in the future (Giri, May 24, 2022). Similarly, Gao Liang, a Nepal researcher at the Institute of South Asian Studies at Sichuan University in China says that Zeya's visit to Tibetan refugee camps is no less than an interference in China's internal affairs. That visit is sure to have many negative effects. Nepal's leaders need to show a long-term vision and a high level of political prudence in this regard (Giri, May 24, 2022).

Zeya has been the most senior US diplomat to visit Nepal since 2012. While in India, she visited Dharamsala and met the Tibetan religious leader, the Dalai Lama. After the details of his visit to Nepal and India became public, the International Campaign for Tibet noted that Tibetan refugees in Nepal were at greater risk owing to pressure from the Chinese government to Nepal (Dahal, May 20, 2022).

President Xi Jinping, also General Secretary of the Communist Party of China Central Committee and Chairman of the Central Military Commission visited Southwest China's Tibet Autonomous Region in May 2021 for the 70th anniversary of Tibet's peaceful liberation (Xuanmin, July 23, 2021). Those three days' visits to Tibet for the first time in three decades will have an impact on Nepal's geopolitics, security, and economy (Dahal, May 25, 2021).

Chinese State Councilor and Foreign Minister Wang Yi, who visited Nepal shortly after Nepal's parliament ratified the MCC agreement, emphasized the importance of bilateral cooperation based on the BRI, but Nepal's Foreign Ministry's statement did not mention BRI. Even after the great interest of China to initiate the BRI projects, but non-fulfillment of its implementation indicate a change in the China policy under the leadership of the Deuba government. China may have an understanding that the non-compliance of the BRI projects happened on the whisper of the US. The cancellation of agreements with a Chinese company for the construction of the Budigandaki Hydropower Project under the leadership of Prime Minister Sher Bahadur Deuba twice and the lack of concrete progress in the Nepal-China railway, power grid, and dry port projects can be taken as examples of the government's changed policy towards China. Hu noted that Nepal's acceptance of the US-funded MCC and its apparent reluctance to pursue BRI programs are indications of some bad warnings for the future (Dahal, May 20, 2022).

Ukraine is supported by the US and the West, and Hong Kong and Taiwan may have received the same assistance in the future. Although Hong Kong and Taiwan are not independent nations like Ukraine, they are integral and inalienable parts of China. But growing tensions with China and US support for Taiwan could make matters worse in this region. Due to the Ukraine issue, the US has imposed strict economic sanctions on Russia but did not directly involve on the battlefield. The same treatment may repeat in the case of Taiwan vs China after the Ukraine-Russia war is over.

Box 1 below shows the people have the right to select their representatives before the election. It seems to indicate a lot as a symbol of present-day Nepal. They may not have believed in Nepal's democratic election because they are accustomed to the culture of Tibet as their trade and customs are more likely to China. Disgusted by Nepal's politics, they want to stay away from the government and the party's culture of dirty politics. Hate politics may have been fuelled further as media quoted that former King Birendra and his family's property have also been delivered to the Yeti which is established under the patronage of UML Chairman KP Oli.

Leaders of political parties have amassed immense wealth for themselves and their families. If the right to reject (as per the decision of the Supreme Court to formulate law on January 9, 2014) (Pant, August 30, 2021) was placed in the ballot papers, more than one-third of the votes would have been cast against such parties and their politicians. The right to reject is a form of protest where the voter stamps no to all the candidates during the voting period in the booth. It is the formal expression of the opinion of voters in the democratic process (Pant, August 30, 2021). Moreover, elections are very expensive. Those who do not have money do not dare to stand as a candidate for the election in Nepal. The wealth of the country has been accumulated by the leaders and those close to him, family, and courtiers.

Electoral Politics Hateism

Limi, the ward no. six of the Namkha Rural Municipality has selected a ward chair and four members by village gatherings or assembly, two months before holding local elections in May 2022. Namkha, the Himalayan region is surrounded by Tibet from the North to the West part of Nepal in the Humla District of Karnali Province. Namkha Municipality Vice-Chairperson Pema Tamang says that the assembly selected the ward representatives to stay away from the dirty politics. Paljor Tamang has been re-selected as the ward chairman. Other all four have been selected as new members. The assembly was convened by one person, the head of the family from each of Limi's houses. The people's representatives were selected in the same way even before the local level elections of 2017. The locals of Limi have their own rules. Meetings of the villagers are held while ploughing the fields and harvesting the grains. No local is allowed to work in the village without the direction of the chairman. Not only public, but also private work requires the permission of the chairperson. Those who fail to attend will have to pay as much as Rs 1,000 to Rs 100,000 Nepalese currency as a fine. The date, time and place of the meeting will be fixed in advance. Only the head of the household above 16 years of age and under 60 years of age can participate in the meeting. The locals of Limi meet every year in November to decide on important issues including the development plans to implement in the village". Lama, Chhapal. (March 20, 2022). ekantipur.com

China still believes that MCC Nepal Compact is not the best of its favour and interest. After the Nepal Compact ratification, large numbers of US spies started to come Nepal in the name of the MCC employees. These employees will be involved in the free Tibet movement. The US and its satellite alliance including NATO will create tensions with China provocating independent Taiwan on the one hand. On the other, the slogan of independent Tibet will soon be rose from the land of Nepal. The process of free Tibet movement will again be resumed two to three times a week in Kathmandu streets similar to the tenure of the United Nations OHCHR and the United Nations Mission in Nepal (UNMIN) were stationed for some years in Kathmandu.

Freedom on Empire of Lie

The Empire of Lie is to discuss how the United States and its military alliance encircle, attack, and destroy its potential rivals or Governments and leaders abusing their powers, including NATO. Before any kind of action against the rivals, the US spreads the jingoistic propaganda itself and even through NATO. NATO is a constituent of a collective, defensive, and rich countries' alliance that mostly functions under the leadership of the US.

The main objective of NATO is to guarantee the security and freedom of its member countries by political-military-triumphalist means. Among the 30 members of NATO, 27 countries are from Europe, one country in Eurasia, and only two in North America (Dixit, May 18, 2022). Eight are the aspiring members of NATO.

NATO was formed in 1949 with 12 founding members as US, UK, France, Belgium, Norway, Denmark, Italy, Netherlands, Luxemburg, Iceland, Denmark, and Canada (Bevans, 1968). It has added new members eight times as of April 2022, when Greece and Turkey became NATO's first two new members in February 1952 since its creation (www.nato.int/cps/fr/natohq/declassified_181434.htm). Similarly, West Germany joined NATO in May 1955 and Spain in 1982 (Barany, 2003).

After the dissolution of the Soviet Union in 1991 called the end of the Cold War I and after the unification of Germany, some former Warsaw Pact and post-Soviet states such as Poland, Hungary, and the Czech Republic (Warsaw Pact countries) initiated discussions about their joining to NATO and formally joined in 1999 (Paquette, 2000 & www.nato.int/docu/presskit/010219/004gb.pdf) amid much debate within NATO members where Russia was a disagree on the decision.

The post-Cold War I membership action plan of NATO seven Central and Eastern Soviet Bloc Baltic countries such as Bulgaria, Estonia, Latvia, Lithuania, Romania, Slovakia, and Slovenia (Inotal, Autumn 2009) joined NATO before Istanbul Summit 2004 (Peter, September 3, 2014) and Romania in March 2004 (NATO, March 2, 2022). Two Albania and Croatia joined NATO in April 2009, Montenegro in June 2017, and North Macedonia in March 2020 (NATO, May 14, 2022).

On May 18, 2022, Finland and Sweden submitted an official application to join NATO (Henley, 2022 & May 18, 2022). Several countries such as Bosnia-Herzegovina, Georgia, and Ukraine are aspiring members of NATO (NATO, May 14, 2022, George & Teigen, January 9, 2009). NATO invited Bosnia-Herzegovina to join it in April 2010 (NATO, May 14, 2022). There is also a debate about Ireland, Moldova, and Serbia in European Countries joining NATO (Lynch, Suzanne, February 11, 2013, Sanchez, January 9, 2013, & UPI November 26, 2013). The US and NATO jointly launched offensive activities against their rival groups in post-Cold War I.

In June 2017, the Ukrainian Parliament adopted legislation reinstating membership in NATO. In 2019, Ukraine entered into force amending its Constitution. In September 2020, President Volodymyr Zelenskyy approved a new National Security Strategy for Ukraine's distinctive partnership with NATO (NATO, March 11, 2022). In response, the Russia-Ukraine conflict started in February 2022 regarding Russia's illegal annexation of Crimea.

NATO has increased its presence in the Black Sea and stepped up maritime cooperation with Ukraine and Georgia (NATO, March 11, 2022). Russia strongly demands to disband NATO in the post-Cold War era. NATO is developed as a US geopolitical and complex superiority body.

On February 24, 2022, the Russian military formally invaded Ukraine accusing Ukraine of being the government of neo-Nazis that being prosecuted the ethnic Russian minority living in Ukraine, but an informal war had begun in 2014 when Russia annexed the Crimea. Russia felt a threat, hostile actions, and isolated and marginalized nation because of the NATO's presence in the Baltic region, missile defense threats, enlargement, and encirclement of it since the early 2000s. Earlier, NATO had promised Russia that its force would not expand in the post-Cold War I period and Russia strongly demanded Georgia and Ukraine would not join NATO (NATO, January 27, 2022).

Thousands of Ukrainian have since died that invasion created Europe's largest refugee crisis since World War II (Keane & Blake, March 14, 2022) where more than 6.3 million Ukrainians fled the neighboring countries (UNHCR, May 19, 2022), a third of the population displaced. Vladimir Putin initiated the biggest war in Europe since World War II justifying that western-leaning-cum-modern Ukraine was a continuous threat to Russia where Russia could not feel "safe, develop, and exist" (Kirby, May 9, 2022).

The US is indirectly assisting in the Ukrainian war. It has been supporting Ukraine by collecting information, spying, and providing necessary information through state-of-the-art digital and satellite technology. Also, new war skills and tactics are being used in this war. That is why Russia felt difficult to surrender to Ukraine.

So the most pressing US strategic-tactical aim of NATO is to confront Russia for soaring oil and gas prices and to harm Germany. In addition to generating profits and stock-market achievements for US oil companies, higher energy demands, and prices will take the steam out of the German economy. In a century, the US will have overwhelmed Germany for the third time, each time increasing its control over the German economy to make more dependent it on the US (Michael, February 28, 2022). To keep Germany under the US's control, the largest in terms of military officials is stationed in Ramstein Air Base comprising 9,200 personnel (Department of Defense, 2016).

Before the attack, the US was pushing Ukraine not to compromise and intimidate the Russian forces. The US President agitated Ukrainian through jingoistic mediaism stating that the US have already sent large numbers of troops and arms and ammunition to help Ukraine. He further claimed more numbers of troops and weapons are coming. When Russia invaded war with Ukraine and the Ukrainians suffered and was victimized a lot, the US did not fulfil its prior promises, similar to proxy warfare statements.

In this war, the US had three objectives: to sell large numbers of weapons and ammunition from its war industries, to weaken Russia without directly involving the US and NATO, to increase the prices of oil and gas, and sell it in Europe. The US succeeded to achieve all the targeted objectives in this Russian-Ukraine war. The UK had been deeply involved in training to forces of Ukraine before the war started (Chatham, May 20, 2022). There has been a lot of disinformation and cyber warfare occurred (Chatham House, May 19, 2022) during between Russia-Ukraine war.

US President Biden has constantly been demanding for over a year to Germany that it needs to stop the Nord Stream 2 pipeline for low-priced gas supplying in its industry and housing but turns to buy much higher-priced US supplying petroleum products. The US tried hard to stop the construction of the pipeline, but Russia completed itself last September (Michael, February 28, 2022). Nord Stream 2 is a 1,200km long pipeline under the Baltic Sea in which gas supplies from Russia to Germany. Before its approval of it, the gas pipeline has been put on hold owing to the Ukraine-Russia war (Ukraine-Russia War, February 2022). The Nord Stream 2 was halted under the pressure of the US stating a National Security threat to the entire Europe from Russia. The US wants retaliation against Germany as the incumbent President Frank-Walter Steinmeier cancelled $ 1 billion in new port facilities for US tanker ships to unload natural gas for Germany and Europe to use after the retirement of Angela Markel.

Even during the Cold War I period, the US adopted several Truman, Kennedy, Carter, Regan, and Bush doctrines. Among them, Regan and Bush had been the most influential US Presidents to launch anti-Communist resistance groups (Pach, March 2006) throughout the world history which later declared Regan-Bush doctrines.

For the specific purpose, the US adopted to embrace change regime, proxy conflicts or wars, espionage, disinformation, and clandestine or suspicious activities within the land and beyond to collapse the communist regimes and satellite communism. After the collapse of the Soviet Union in 1991, the US appeared as the world's sole superpower that continuously intervened in Africa, Eastern Europe, the Middle East, and others as it wishes.

Against the seven months long Iraqi military occupation in Kuwait, the US-led coalition, principal NATO members (Gause, Undated) intervened in Kuwait called Gulf War in February 1991 and succeeded to drive out the Iraqi forces (Freedman and Karsh, 1991). As per Shia and Kurdish demands, the coalition intervened and created no-fly zones that subsequently granted autonomy to the Kurds (Romano, 2010).

Twelve years later, the US-led forces invaded Iraq in March 2003 (Congressional Research Service, June 5, 2020) again that lasted for 22 days. The invaded forces captured the capital city of Baghdad on April 9, 2003, after the six-day-long Battle at Baghdad (Hornick, November 18, 2010).

The coalition partners such as US President Bush and UK PM Tony Blair purposively aimed to disarm Iraq through mass destruction and to end terrorism supported by Saddam Hussein in the name to make free Iraqi people (The White House, March 22, 2003, & 2001).

However, the UN Inspection Team had neither found evidence of the existence of weapons of mass destruction nor supported testimonies of terrorism by Saddam Hussein (SC/7777, June 5, 2003). Eminent Chip Pitts comments, "The American empire sits, naked, exposed, and somewhat battered, in Iraq's hot desert sun. Whereas American power had largely been seen before as benevolent, cooperative, and based on shared values and institutions, George W. Bush's misadventure in Iraq has changed that for at least a generation and perhaps forever" (Pitts, August 11, 2006).

President Bush's administration had made a total of 935 false speeches in two years having Iraq's alleged threat to the US (News, January 23, 2008). The CIA was involved in the 1996 coup against Saddam Hussein, but it failed (Association of Former Intelligence Officers, May 19, 2003).

While lethal weapons and weapons of mass destruction did not find, the United States and NATO accepted the fact that the issue as an unintentional mistake. They dismissed the facts of extrajudicial killings, disappearances, inhuman tortures of children and Iraqi people, destruction public and private properties, and infrastructures there. The truth is that people often advocate on victim justice and the

International Criminal Court. But, the history has been a witness of that the US is on the side of the victors' justice further victimizing and suffering the victims.

Against the September 11, 2001 attacks (Smith & Zeigler, 2017), the Bush administration combined US led (including NATO) launched the global War on Terror with the purpose to depose the Taliban Government in Afghanistan with a suspicious of protecting al-Qaeda and the Islamic State (CBS News, September 12, 2021). The War on Terror aimed to dismantle international counterterrorism and other extreme institutions or groups.

The War on Terror represented a new phase of international-political relations in the world and it has given sharp consequences for human security, human rights, governance, development cooperation, and international law. The war on terror was sharply criticized even by the US senior security personnel such as four-star retired General Richard B. Myers, Chairman of the Joint Chiefs of Staff, and many others (Ambinder, May 20, 2010).

On May 23, 2012, US President Barrack Obama avoided the use of the term announcing the Global War on Terror was over (The Washington Times, August 6, 2009). Even though, Obama ordered a surge in US forces to Afghanistan deploying an additional 30,000 troops to fight against al-Qaeda and the Taliban insurgency in December 2009 (Mount, September 21, 2012). The US and NATO war on terror continued until 2021. The war in Afghanistan became the longest war in US history lasting 19 years and 10 months whereas the Vietnam War lasted for 19 years and five months with a cost of US $ 2 trillion (Ojeda, August 15, 2021).

The research of the Watson Institute for International and Public Affairs, Brown University conducted in 2021 criticized the war on terror questioning its morality, efficiency, and cost. The several post-9/11 wars participated in the war on terror (war against terror) have caused 38 million people displaced in Afghanistan, Pakistan, Iraq, Libya, Syria, Yemen, Somalia, and the Philippines, but only 26.7 million people have returned home (Vine, et al, August 19, 2021). The research estimated those wars caused the killings of 897,000 to 929,000 people including US military members, allied fighters, opposition fighters, civilians, journalists, and humanitarian aid workers (Kimball, September 1, 2021).

Those wars also included over 364,000 civilians that cost the US $8 trillion (Crawford, September 1, 2021, and Crawford & Lutz, September 1, 2021). Over 2,400 US military, 18 CIA operatives, and over 1,800 civilian contractors were killed in the Afghan War (DeLuca and Straight, September 21, 2021).

On August 15, 2021, Former Senior US Army Officer and Senator Richard Ojeda criticized through a tweet, "2 trillion dollars to train and equip the Afghan military over the past 20 years.... It was about military contractors and corporations raking in the profits. I am numb. I am sure everyone who spent years there feels the same!" (Ojeda, August 15, 2021).

What about the costs for the future care of veterans? If the US had spent such 2 trillion dollars in the name of humanitarianism for the Afghan people, those people neither go against the US nor the Taliban have reoccupied Afghanistan before the US and NATO military alliance left Kabul last year. As long as the US citizens are there, they will continuously ask a question with the regimes, 'why had the Government spent a large amount of money for such an unsuccessful war in Afghanistan in the name of freedom?

Libya is mostly a desert and oil-rich country that had been ruled for the 42-year (1969-2011) by the mercurial Colonel

Muammar Gaddafi. He was extrajudicially killed in October 2011 following an armed rebellion assisted, promoted, and protected by the Western military intervention (Libya Crisis, March 15, 2021). Gaddafi was killed from bullet wounds sometimes after a failed attempt to escape from the insurgents and the NATO forces.

A group carrying Gaddafi and his loyalists was destroyed by a French fighter jet (NEWS Africa, May 23, 2022). He had been charged with violence, instability, and no authority in full control in Libya (BBC News, August 15, 2018). President Reagan intended to kill Gaddafi branding him the "mad dog of the Middle East" (Asser, October 21, 2011).

Cross-party Foreign Affairs Committee, 'House of Commons' of Parliament of United Kingdom conducted an in-depth investigation and released its report on September 6, 2016 (HC119, September 6, 2016). The report strongly condemned the British' government's role in the Libya intervention detailing how NATO's 2011 war in Libya was based on lies.

The report further stated that Gaddafi was not going to massacre civilians, but Western bombing made Islamist extremism worse (Norton, September 16, 2016). The report highlighted how France's motives had been to overthrow Gaddafi's rule to increase its share of Libya's oil production, reinforce French influence in Africa, and recover President Sarkozy's position at home. It further stated how Islamic extremists had an excessive influence on the uprising but that was largely ignored by the West (Dewan, September 14, 2016).

Opposing the US military intervention in Libya, US Libertarian Party's statement said, "President Obama's decision to order military attacks on Libya is only surprising to those who think he deserved the Nobel Peace

Prize. He has now ordered bombing strikes in six different countries, adding Libya to Afghanistan, Iraq, Pakistan, Somalia, and Yemen". Ralph Nader, a former Green Party presidential candidate stated President Obama was a war criminal and called for his impeachment. Similarly, Congressman Dennis Kucinich talked of impeachment. Michael Moore vented his spleen on the subject of US hypocrisy (Avlon, March 23, 2011).

At the end of the Cold War I and post-Cold War I periods, the US had already initiated the proliferation of war industries through foreign intervention. War industry is the principal income of the US and then oil-and-gas companies, drug manufacturers, share markets, and cigarette productions respectively. This means to produce much more wars in the world pretending democratic establishment, human rights compliance, war on terror, identity respect (autonomy), protection of the minority, assistance, and among others.

US military warfare and intervention have almost failed worldwide ranging from Vietnam to Cuba and Venezuela to Afghanistan while the dissidents adopted a guerilla warfare defense policy of 'assembling the parts into a whole for action and 'dispersing the whole into parts' after the completion of the action. Since then, the US has succeeded in establishing its puppet governments in many countries waging war against dissident forces, either to prove its superiority and control of resources or for the flourishing of the arms industry.

Meanwhile, NATO has also distributed one and a half times more membership in three decades of post-Cold War I. Such proliferation of such membership is itself an example of imposition of fear psychology. The 'divide and rule' and 'the enemy of my enemy is my friend' are the core policies of the empire of lies (US and NATO expanders) around the world.

On the fifth day of the MCC was ratified, Nepal voted in favor of the UN resolution against the Russian invasion of Ukraine. But, Nepal lies in between two emerging superpowers, i.e., China and India, but both are still (at the end of May 2022) neutral in the case of the Ukraine-Russia war. US Air Force aircraft landed at Kathmandu International Airport for the third time in a year within 20 days of MCC approval. Nepalis have doubted whether the tools to encircle China for the autonomous Tibet were brought on board. In its 26 days of MCC ratification, Nepal voted at the UNGA against the humanitarian crisis in Ukraine. Those all happened during PM Deuba's tenure.

A three-day official visit of a four US Congressional Delegation, headed by Senator Kristen Gillibrand arrived in Nepal in less than two months of MCC endorsement. Less than three months after the MCC approval, the US Under Secretary Uzra Zeya came to Nepal for three days (May 20-22, 2022) official visit to understand Tibetan refugees residing in Nepal since along. This means that the Deuba government has come closer to US satellite ruling ignoring Nepal is sandwiched between two giant emerging superpowers, i.e., China and India.

On the other hand, Nepal's border with China is 1,414 km long. There are potentially advanced the Cold War II because of the US-India and China informal and formal conflicts on the course to control weak, poor, small, landlocked, and underdeveloped country Nepal. The common Nepali has a view that the US granted MCC for Nepal may not be sole economic cooperation and assistance alone as the US has a history of an empire of lies. The common character of an empire of lies headed by the US is, "does not do what it says; does not say what it does".

Conclusion

There had been intense protests and arguments of the MCC every talk from center to village to towns, namely, *Chowk* (crossroad/Bazar), Chautari (rest place), schools, teashops, offices, leaders' speeches, both print, and online media, social media, radio, and Television among others and every professional before the ratification of the MCC in Nepal. Activists blindly support and follow their leaders. Even if the leaders wrongly addressed, blind devotees of the party spread the message accordingly without reading, asking, and discussing its pros and cons. The ratification of the Nepal Compact formally ends a chaotic five-year-long saga and a political football. Similar to a gun that does not recognize its master, family, relatives, among others; the US can do anything to keep being itself the only superpower in the universe.

MCC is an investment in Nepal. Anti-US forces for instance Communists, royalists, and pro-Chinese commentators were amalgamated to wage a rhetorical warfare against the Nepal Compact grant. They deliberately used social media campaigns against the motive of the Indo-Pacific Strategy.

The one-side-fits-all protest has shocked development partners on the one hand and reached public outcry and controversy over the US policy on the other. Some of these protests have and had been a source of frustration against the United States rather than providing the right information. Few have had to please China and pursue their interests. Many protest the Nepal Compact because of its anti-India and anti-US sentiment. Whatever the purpose of the MCC, there has been a major shift in public sentiment to see, watch, and evaluate the United States. A great number of grass-root level people believe that the ratification of the Nepal Compact is to invite the US troops in the name of a grant in Nepal. The impression on the local people is that what the United States had been, is, and will be doing in Nepal is based on the policy of encircling China using Nepal's land rather than on humanism. It will take a long time to change the feelings on the US in Nepal.

It is not only the fault of Nepalis to see and understand MCC along this negative way of line. This means, that to develop the negative sentiments among the populace there has been a higher role of the US and those Nepali elites who are close to its power, property, and politics and advocate for it. The common mass has an understanding that the United States rules all poor countries through satellite by protecting, promoting, lifting, and embracing the limited elite ones. Why don't Nepalis trust America? There are several reasons.

First, in 1980, Rapti Rural Area Development Project (RADP) launched an agricultural research and extension program in the Rapti zone (Gow, May 1980 and Skerry, Moran, & Calavan, 1992) for 15 years at the cost of $28.8 million (Final Evaluation: February 1995). The People's War started in the same area within one and half months (43 days) of the completion of the project funded by USAID, suggesting that the project protected the elites only. The CPN (Maoist) initiated the People's War on February 13, 1996, with the main objectives of sweeping away the constitutional monarchy, bureaucratic capitalism, feudalistic mode of society (semi-feudalism, semi-imperialism, and capitalism), and historical roots of social inequality to establish a patriotic, democratic, progressive, and prosperous People's Republic of Nepal (Pathak, 2005).

Second, the delegation team of the United People's Front (UPF) – a youth wing of the revolutionary Maoist party – submitted a petition of 40-point demands to the then PM

95

Sher Bahadur Deuba on February 2, 1996, with an ultimatum of 15 days to respond to or to accept the demands. However, the UPF announced the beginning of the People's War four days earlier than the proposed deadline, the day following the signing of the controversial Integrated Mahakali Treaty in New Delhi on February 12, 1996, by Sher Bahadur Deuba and his Indian counterpart PV Narasimha Rao (Bagale and Adhikari, 2020). The numbers 6 and 9 of the demands concerning nationality said, "Abolish monopoly of foreign capital in Nepali economy" and "Stop imperialist/hegemonic encroachment through NGOs and INGOs". Those two demands were particularly designed against the US. During the People's War period (1996-2006), the Americans used to visit Nepal in the name of British people while the Maoists primarily targeted the US citizens and their projects across Nepal.

Third, in April 2008's Constituent Assembly Elections, the former insurgent People's War, emerged at the top of the results of the election receiving 53 percent (119 seats out of 224), whereas NC, UML, and Madhesi Janadhikar Forum (MJF) got 15, 14 and 11 percent respectively in the first-past-the-post election. Since the restoration of democracy in Nepal in 1990, many anti-American and anti-Indian sentiments carriers have won the General Elections (Pathak, May 8, 2008).

Fourth, the USAID recruits its loyal 'yes-man' rather than selecting capable and good people for all its development projects. These people have neither the professional ethics and academic abilities nor the capacity to analyze potential future consequences. Moreover, such people often have an absence of influential personality and prestige. As a result, its grant programs have become divisive and have created a bad image among the people. The same trend also grows in partner selection in NGOs, which has created a huge gap between haves and haves not. The protest against Nepal

Compact is just a symbolic one. Most of such employees disappear from the social welfare sphere from the day they finish their term of job positions or the US carries on them in their country, the US.

Fifth, Nepal's a few communists and a large number of *kamaunists* (earnings for himself, family, coterie/own faction, and then own-party, respectively) distribute their election manifestos from center to village and then community. They attract voter-banks (poor voters) with high hopes and expectations with the idea of social justice and egalitarian society establishing socialism, sharply revoking and criticizing the United States just to win the elections. The abusive attitude started by the parties against the US is not limited to the cadres but reach voter at the grassroots level in Nepal. Even if the United States has a program with good intentions and humanitarian motions, negative discussion initiates here, there, and everywhere. The author has not been seen any effort of the US to improve its image and to clean its black cloud among the Nepali people. Rather than its clarification, it only serves to a few elites that further alienate its opponents.

Sixth, on March 18, 2022, a US Air Force aircraft landed at Tribhuvan International Airport, Kathmandu at 9 O'clock for the fourth time in 14 months. Such army ships arrived in January, April, and August of 2021 previously. The military ship was used to carry on US diplomats, essential goods, and documents for the US Embassy in Kathmandu (www.onlinekhabar.com/2022/03/1095468 & www.dcnepal.com/2022/03/340489/). The sudden landing of a US military aircraft in Nepal just 19 days after the Nepal Compact approval has strengthened the voices of Nepalis who time and again stated that ratifying the MCC is the arrival of US troops in Nepal. On the other hand, Nepalis believe that US military forces along with weapons and related tools were landed in Kathmandu in the names of diplomats goods.

The history reveals that the main source of America has been to sell arms and ammunition to the countries that are competing neighbors. If the countries fail to wage war, the US becomes involved on this and that matters, so ultimately the war initiates. Nepalis are afraid of whether Nepal is moving in the same direction. Nepali people's suspicions were further enriched during the four day (June 9-12, 2022) official visits of Commanding General of the US Army Pacific Charles A. Flynn, proposing an agreement of State Partnership Program to the PM Deuba and Chief of the Army Staff. A state partnership program (SPP) is a component of the IPS.

But, both consciously replied, "Both the prime minister and the army chief are seeking a broader political consensus for signing the agreement. If there is consensus, then Nepal will possibly sign the agreement during Prime Minister Deuba's visit to the US in July" 2022 (Giri, June 11, 2022). The Army Chief General Sharma is visiting the US after June 27, 2022. The leaders, lawmakers, media, foreign-security experts, and civil society are presenting their arguments on the SPP. On June 15, 2022, Manuel P. Micaller, Deputy Chief of Mission at the US Embassy in Kathmandu briefing the media said, "after Nepal applied for SSP in 2015 and 2017, we finally accepted the request in 2019" (english.khabarhub.com/2022/15/257765/).

The poor people of the village believe in their self-esteem and respect rather than in anyone's hopes and trust. Taking advantage of the straightforwardness of the poor people, a few socio-politics professionals use them as their personal property. Some of them succeed to gain the position showing their competence at their respective leaders. The leaders make public speeches considering America as their main imperialist enemy during the day, but at night or in secret, they praise America to continuously stay in power or to grasp the state power and to earn a huge sum of money. Despite Nepal being rich in terms of geographical verities and resources, when will the slave-minds of such (proxy, doubled-edge sword, and eunuch) leaders be liberated?

The role of the CPN (UML) is similar to the eunuch. While in the government, the UML tried hard to ratify the Nepal Compact. When almost two-thirds Oli-led communist Government became an opposition party due to incompetence to rule Nepal, its obstructions to the House continued even on the day the MCC was being ratified.

Those who studied deeply at the MCC raised several constraints about it. Dr. Bhim Rawal, Jhalnath Khanal among others advocated lot for not to ratify the Nepal Compact unless it shall have necessary amendments. A few those who studied a little had confusion and those who did not have the time and ability to study, were supported the MCC whole-heartily.

We already live in a Global village where each individual and land is connected by digital highways. The good is that Nepal is in between two giants Dragon (China) and Elephant (India). The bad part is that Nepal is in the deep shadow similar to the bottom of the candle of two emerging superpowers. The irony is that China is in a favor of a strong, stable, prosperous, and developed Nepal whereas India desires to have a weak, poor, unstable, and underdeveloped country for the sake to control Nepal and its natural resources, i.e., Pancheshwar multipurpose project which was signed 26 years ago, but progress is zero as of May 2022.

Whether China and US-India develop cordial friendship, compete with one another, and live in a potential for Cold War II phase, Nepal will only be the country that faces a severe crisis in all dimensions, specifically in a politico-economy battleground. Now the US puts pressure on Nepal to provide testimonies or documents of Tibetan refugees residing in Nepal while China has started putting pressure not to provide any testimonies to them. In the end, it is Nepal that suffers from both competing superpowers. Thus, the initiation of MCC projects in Nepal will surely invite potential Cold War II.

**

Annex – I: Joint Letter to the MCC Board

September 29, 2021

The Chairman,
Millennium Challenge Corporation Board 1099 Fourteenth
Street NW
Washington, DC 20005 United State of America

Ref: **MCC Compact with Nepal and
Ratification**

Dear Chairman,

We convey our warm greetings and best wishes to the Government and the people of the United States of America.

We acknowledge with appreciation the Millennium Challenge Compact signed between the United States of America, acting through the MCC and Federal Democratic Republic of Nepal acting through Ministry of Finance dated September 14, 2017 (the "Compact"); and The Program Implementation Agreement signed on September 29, 2019 (the "PIA").

In this context, we, Sher Bahadur Deuba, Prime Minister and President of the Nepali Congress and Pushpa Kamal Dahal 'Prachanda', Chairman of the Communist Party of Nepal (Maoist Center), leaders of the coalition partners of the present Government of Nepal, jointly make request to the MCC Board for providing additional time for the ratification of the Compact.

Detailed discussions were held a n d we conveyed our commitment to ratification during the recent visit of Ms

Fartema Z. Sumar, Vice President, Compact Operations. The newly formed coalition government is making all efforts possible towards this end.

We want to assure you of Government of Nepal's interest in securing the MCC grant and implementing it for the economic development of Nepal.

To demonstrate our commitment to the MCC compact, we agree to the following actions to be taken in the next four-five months with the goal of securing required majority in the House of Representatives for the ratification of the Compact. We specifically commit to:

- discuss the clarifications received from MCC with all the coalition Partners to better inform our party members,

- use Government of Nepal resources to communicate publicly with the Nepali people and state the Government's support for implementing the Compact and to dispel misunderstandings and apprehensions about the Compact,

- hold a joint press conference with leaders of the coalition partners to demonstrate Government's positive views on the MCC ratification,

- disseminate accurate information about the Compact through state media,

- encourage the MCA-Nepal to complete technical and communication activities that will allow the Compact to be implemented more quickly, and

- jointly request the Speaker of the House of Representatives to plan for tabling of the Compact for the ratification as soon as possible.

We believe completing these activities will help make possible garnering required parliamentary majority for the ratification of the Compact in the next four-five months.

In view of the foregoing and in consideration of the long standing friendship and cooperation that exists between our two countries and peoples, we believe that our request for addition time for ratification will be accepted by the MCC Board.

We look forward to receiving positive response at the earliest opportunity.

Sincerely yours,

Sher Bahadur Deuba,

Prime Minister and President,

Nepali Congress

Puspa Kamal Dahal 'Prachanda'

Former Prime Minister and Chairman

Communist Party of Nepal (Maoist Center)

About the Author

Transnational Professor Bishnu Pathak was a former Senior Commissioner at the Commission of Investigation on Enforced Disappeared Persons (CIEDP), Nepal who has been a Noble Peace prize nominee 2013-2019 for his noble finding of Peace-Conflict Lifecycle similar to the ecosystem. A Board Member of the TRANSCEND Peace University holds a Ph.D. in interdisciplinary Conflict Transformation and Human Rights in about two decades. Arduous Dr. Pathak who is an author of over 100 international paper-book publications has been used as a reference in more than 100 countries across the globe. Immense versatile personality Mr. Pathak's publications belong to Human Rights, Peace, Conflict Transformation, and Transitional Justices among others.

Abbreviations

B3W	Build Back Better World
BBC	British Broadcasting Corporation
BDN	Blue Dot Network
BRI	Belt and Road Initiative
CEO	Chief Executive Officer
CPN	Communist Party of Nepal
DAC	Development Assistance Committee
G7	Group of Seven
IPS	Indo-Pacific Strategy
MCA	Millennium Challenge Account
MCC	Millennium Challenge Corporation
MDGS	Millennium Development Goals
MJF	Madhesi Janadhikar Forum
MoU	Memorandum of Understanding
NATO	North Atlantic Treaty Organization
NC	Nepali Congress
NGO	Non-Government Organization
OBOR	One Belt One Road
OECD	Organization for Economic Cooperation and Development
OHCHR	Office of High Commission for Human Rights
PM	Prime Minister
RADP	Rapti Rural Area Development Project
THT	The Himalayan Times
TTA	Transit Transport Agreement
UML	United Marxist-Leninist

UN	United Nations
UNGA	United Nations General Assembly
UNMIN	United Mission to Nepal
UPF	United People's Front
US	United States
USAID	United States Agency for International Development

References

1. A/RES/55/2. (2000, September 18). *55/2: United Nations Millennium Declaration.* New York: Fifty-fifth Session of General Assembly.

2. Aamir, Adnan. (2021, November 30). "China-Pakistan Belt and Road Initiative hits buffers". *NIKKEI Asia.* Retrieved April 16, 2022, from https://asia.nikkei.com/Spotlight/Asia-Insight/China-Pakistan-Belt-and-Road-Initiative-hits-buffers.

3. Acharya, Puspa Raj. (2017, September 15). "Nepal, United States sign $500m grant agreement". *The Himalayan Times.* Kathmandu.

4. Adhikary, Ashis. (2022). "Millennium Challenge Corporation: Interpretations and Implications for the National Security of Nepal". *Unity Journal.* Volume III. https://doi.org/10.3126/unityj.v3i01.43314.

5. Aditya, Ananda. (2022, February 20). "The USA values our strategic space, China seeks stake building. Kathmandu:*Nepal Khabar*. Retrieved April 30, 202, from nepalkhabar.com/interview/121042-2022-2-18-17-59-41.

6. Ambinder, Marc. (2010, May 20). "The New Term for the War on Terror". *The Atlantic.* Retrieved May 21, 2022, from www.theatlantic.com/politics/archive/2010/05/the-new-term-for-the-war-on-terror/56969/.

7. *Ameriki Airforcedko Jahaj Kathmanduma (US Air Force Aircraft in Kathmandu).* Retrieved April

22, 2022, from https://www.onlinekhabar.com/2022/03/1095468.

8. *An Agreement of MCC-Nepal Compact.* (2017, September). Washington: MCC Headquarters.

9. ANI. (2022, April 12). "Sri Lanka temporarily suspends servicing USD 51 billion foreign debt payments". *The Print.* Retrieved April 16, 2022, from https://theprint.in/world/sri-lanka-temporarily-suspends-servicing-usd-51-billion-foreign-debt-payments/913054/.

10. *Annapurna Express.* (2022, February 18). "China opposes 'coercive diplomacy' of US in pushing MCC compact in Nepal". Kathmandu: Annapurna Media Network. Retrieved April 4, 2022, from https://theannapurnaexpress.com/news/china-opposes-coercive-diplomacy-of-us-in-pushing-mcc-compact-in-napal-4497.

11. *Annapurna Post.* (2022, February 16). "MCCrokna Prachandako Dawab, Pradhanmantri Deuba Byak Nahune (Prachanda's Pressure to Stop MCC, Prime Minister Deuba will not Back). Kathmandu: Annapurna Media Network.

12. Asser, Martin. (2011, October 21). "The Muammar Gaddafi story". *BBC News.* Retrieved May 23, 2022, from www.bbc.com/news/world-africa-12688033

13. Association of Former Intelligence Officers. (2003, May 19). *Weekly Intelligence Notes # 19-03.* Retrieved May 20, 2022, from https://www.afio.com/sections/wins/2003/2003-19.html#terrirst

14. Avlon, John p. (2011, March 23). "Left's view on Libya: Is this Bush's third term?". *CNN.* Retrieved

May 23, 2022, from
edition.cnn.com/2011/OPINION/03/23/avlon.left.
obama/

15. Bagale, Dharma R. and Adhikari, Keshab D.
     (2020). Mahakali Treaty: delay in implementation
     and resulting impacts from Nepal's perspective.
     *Water Policy: Official Journal of the World Water
     Council.* Volume 22, Issue 4. Doi:
     doi.org/10.2166/wp.2020.141

16. Barany, Zoltan. (2003). *The Future of NATO
     Expansion: Four Case Studies.* Cambridge
     University Press.

17. BBC News. (2006, April 24). *Full text: King
     Gyanendra's speech.* Retrieved April 8, 2022,
     from
     news.bbc.co.uk/2/hi/south_asia/4940876.stm.

18. BBC News. (2018, August 15*). Libyan court
     sentences 45 to death over 2011 killings.*
     Retrieved May 23, 2022, from
     www.bbc.com/news/world-africa-45203473.

19. Bevans, Charles Irving. (1968). "North Atlantic
     Treaty". *Treaties and other international
     agreements of the United States of America 1776–
     1949.* Vol. 4, Multilateral 1946–1949.
     Washington, D.C.

20. Bhattarai, Kamal Dev. (2019, June 2). "Nepal's
     BRI journey: Heavy on promises, light on
     substance". *The   Annapurna   Express.*
     Kathmandu.

21. Biden, Joe. (2021, October 24). *Indo-Pacific
     Strategy of the United States of America.*
     Washington: The White House.

22. Biden, Joe. (2021, September 21). *The future of each our nations- and indeed the World- depends on a free and open Pacific ending and Indoflourishing in the decades ahead.* Quad Leaders' Summit. Retrieved My 9, 2022, from www.whitehouse.gov/wp-content/uploads/2022/02/U.S.-Indo-Pacific-Strategy.pdf.

23. Bloomberg, Kai Schultz. (2022, April 28). "The Powerful Rajapaksa Dynasty Bankrupted Sri Lanka In Just 30 Months". *NDTV*. Retrieved May 4, 2022, from https://www.ndtv.com/world-news/the-powerful-rajapaksa-dynasty-bankrupted-sri-lanka-in-just-30-months-2927466

24. Blue Dot Network. (2022, March 8). "China's Fears of an Indo-Pacific NATO Are More Myth Than Reality". Retrieved May 8, 2022, from https://www.bloomberg.com/news/articles/2022-03-08/china-s-fears-of-an-indo-pacific-nato-are-more-myth-than-reality.

25. Bonnart, Frederick. (2004, June 26). "Istanbul Summit : NATO could find its new purpose in Iraq". *The New York Times*. Retrieved May 17, 2022, from https://www.nytimes.com/2004/06/26/opinion/IHT-istanbul-summit-nato-could-find-its-new-purpose-in-iraq.html.

26. CBS News. (2021, September 12*). "Countdown bin Laden": Obama's pursuit of the 9/11 mastermind.* Retrieved May 21, 22, from https://www.cbsnews.com/news/chris-wallace-countdown-bin-laden-the-pursuit-of-al-qaeda-leader-osama-bin-laden/.

27. Chand, Hari P. (2021, August). "Nepal's Engagement in BRI and MCC: Implications on Nepal's Geopolitics and Foreign Policy. *Journal of Political Science*. Volume 21, Special Issue.

28. *Chatham House*. (2022, May 20). "War on Ukraine: an assessment of the military and political role of the UK". Retrieved May 22, 2022, from www.chathamhouse.org/events/all/members-event/war-ukraine-assessment-military-and-political-role-uk?

29. *Congressional Research Service*. (2020, June 5). "U.S. Periods of War Recent Conflicts". Retrieved May 21, 2022, from https://sgp.fas.org/crs/natsec/RS21405.pdf.

30. Cormann, Mathias. (2021, June 7). "Inaugural Meeting of the Blue Dot Network's Executive Consultation Group, 7 June 2021". *OECD Home*. Retrieved May 9, 2022, from https://www.oecd.org/about/secretary-general/oecd-sg-remarks-at-blue-dot-network-meeting-7-june-2021.htm

31. Crawford, Neta C. (2021, September 1). "The U.S. Budgetary Costs of the Post-9/11 Wars". *Watson Institute for International and Public Affairs*. Brown University.

32. Crawford, Neta C. and Lutz, Catherine. (2021, September 1). "Human Cost of Post-9/11 Wars: Direct War Deaths in Major War Zones". *Watson Institute for International and Public Affairs*. Brown University.

33. CrowdReviews.com. (2019, March 25). *Over 1,700 projects worth USD 1 trillion fall under China's ambitious One Belt, One Road Initiative*

(OBOR): Annual Investment Meeting 2019 to host AIM-OBOR Forum. Retrieved May 5, 2022, from www.pr.com/press-release/780645.

34. DAC-OECD. (1996, May). *Shaping the 21st Century: The Contribution of Development Co-operation.* Paris: OECD.

35. Dahal, Fanindra. (2022, May 20). "Tibati Mamila Herne Ameriki Kutnitigyako Nepal Bhraman Prati Chinko Chaso (China's Interest in US Diplomat Visit in Nepal)". BBC Nepali News. Retrieved May 28, 2022, from www.bbc.com/nepali/news-61511336.

36. Dahal, Kishor. (2021, April 21). "MCC is successful in 80% countries, Sri Lanka's case is different: CEO of MCA Nepal". *nepalpress.* Retrieved March 30, 2022, from https://english.nepalpress.com/2021/04/21/mcc-is-successful-in-80-countries-sri-lankas-case-is-exceptional-ceo-of-mca-nepal/.

37. *Declaration.* Retrieved April 12, 2022, from www.merriam-webster.com/dictionary/declaration.

38. DeLuca, Zach and Straight, Trenton. (2021, September 21). *Did the U.S. spend $2 trillion to support the Afghan military?* Retrieved May 22, 2022, from https://www.politifact.com/factchecks/2021/sep/21/richard-ojeda/did-us-spend-2-trillion-support-afghan-military/

39. Department of Defense. (2019, June 1). *Indo-Pacific Strategy Report: Preparedness, Partnerships, and Promoting a Networked Region.* Washington. Retrieved May 8, 2022, from

media.defense.gov/2019/Jul/01/2002152311/-1/-1/1/DEPARTMENT-OF-DEFENSE-INDO-PACIFIC-STRATEGY-REPORT-2019.PDF.

40.   Department of Defense. (2015). *Base Structure Report: Fiscal Year 2015 Baseline*. Washington.

41.   Department of State. (2017, November 4). *A Free and Open Indo-Pacific: Advancing a Shared Vision*. Washington: The White House.

42.   Devine, James J.; essay. (March 25, 2011). "Voice of the People: This Used To Be a Free Country". *NJToday.net*.

43.   Dewan, Angela. (2016, September 14). "Britain's Libya intervention led to growth of ISIS, inquiry finds". *CNN*. Retrieved May 23, 2022, from edition.cnn.com/2016/09/13/europe/libya-uk-intervention/index.html

44.   Dixit, Rajni. (2022, May 18). *Nato Countries List 2022 – What & How Powerful Is Nato?* Retrieved May 18, 2022, from dmerharyana.org/nato-countries-list/.

45.   *Ethiopia Proposed Threshold Program*. Retrieved March 30, 2022, from www.mcc.gov/where-we-work/program/ethiopia-proposed-threshold-program.

46.   Explained Desk. (2020, February 26). 'Explained: What is the Blue Dot network, on the table during Trump visit to India'. *The Indian Express*. Retrieved March 18, 2022, from https://indianexpress.com/article/explained/explained-what-is-the-blue-dot-network-on-the-table-during-trump-visit-to-india-6286524/

47.   Final Evaluation. (1995, February). *The Rapti Development Project*. USAID/Nepal, John Mellor

Associates, Inc. and Institute for Integrated Development Studies.

48.   Fishbein, Robert and Haile, Stephanie. (2012). *Principles into Practice: Irrigated Agriculture.* Washington: Millennium Challenge Corporation.

49.   Freedman, Lawrence and Karsh, Efraim. (1991). "How Kuwait Was Won: Strategy in the Gulf War". *International Security*. Vol. 16, No. 2 . doi.org/10.2307/2539059.

50.   Gause, F. Gregory. (Undated). *Iraq and the Gulf War: Decision-Making in Baghdad*. University of Vermont. Retrieved May 21, 2022, from https://www.files.ethz.ch/isn/6844/doc_6846_290 _en.pdf

51.   George, J & Teigen, JM. (2009, January 9). " NATO Enlargement and Institution Building: Military Personnel Policy Challenges in the Post-Soviet Context ". *European Security*. Volume 17 (2-3).

52.   Ghimire, Binod. (2020, January 9). "Why the MCC compact courted controversy in Nepal". *The Kathmandu Post*. Kathmandu: Kantipur Media Group.

53.   Ghimire, Binod. (2022, February 28). "What's in the declaration that led to parliamentary passage of US grant. *The Kathmandu Post*. Kathmandu: Kantipur Media Group.

54.   Ghlionn, John Mac. (2022, February 28). "Analysis: Nepal is torn between a generous 'American gift' and China's BRI". *TRT World*. Retrieved   April   18,   2022,   from https://www.trtworld.com/magazine/analysis-nepal-

is-torn-between-a-generous-american-gift-and-china-s-bri-55162

55. Giri, Anil. (2017, May 9). "Nepal to sign framework deal on OBOR". *The Kathmandu Post*. Kathmandu.

56. Giri, Anil. (2019, January 18). "Nepal trims projects under BRI from 35 to 9 at Chinese call". *The Kathmandu Post*. Kathmandu: Kantipur Media Group.

57. Giri, Anil. (2019, June 19). "For the first time, ruling party lawmakers criticise Oli administration's foreign policy". *The Kathmandu Post*. Kathmandu: Kantipur Media Group.

58. Giri, Anil. (2019, May 15). "Indo-Pacific Strategy is not against any country, visiting US official asserts". *The Kathmandu Post*. Kathmandu: Kantipur Media Group.

59. Giri, Anil. (2019, October 14). "Xi departs, after signing over two dozen agreements and memorandums". *The Kathmandu Post*. Kathmandu: Kantipur Media Group.

60. Giri, Anil. (2022, May 26). "China nudges Nepal on One-China policy". *The Kathmandu Post*. Kathmandu: Kantipur Media Group.

61. Giri, Anil. (2022, June 11). "Visiting US general urges Nepal to join State Partnership Program, promises aid". *The Kathmandu Post*. Kathmandu: Kantipur Media Group.

62. Giri, Sanjib. (2022, May 24). "Nepal-China relations: Is Kathmandu trying to keep distance itself from Beijing? Questions raised by the US Secretary of State during his visit to the Tibetan refugee camp". *BBC Nepali News*. Retrieved May

26, 2022, from www.bbc.com/nepali/news-61539847.

63. *Global Health Policy*. (2019, September 4). "The Millennium Challenge Corporation (MCC) and Global Health". Retrieved April 7, 2022, from https://www.kff.org/global-health-policy/fact-sheet/the-millennium-challenge-corporation-mcc-and-global-health/.

64. *Global Times*. (2022, February 18). "China opposes 'coercive diplomacy' of US in pushing MCC compact in Nepal". Retrieved May 25, 2022,   from https://www.globaltimes.cn/page/202202/125259 7.shtml

65. *Global Times*. (2022, February 23). How can US 'gift' to Nepal be delivered by ultimatum, asks Chinese FM. Retrieved May 26, 2022.

66. Gould, Joe. (2016, June 8). "US Names India 'Major Defense Partner'". *DefenseNews*. Retrieved May 8, 2022, from https://www.defensenews.com/home/2016/06/07/u s-names-india-major-defense-partner/.

67. Government of Nepal. (1990). *Nepal Treaty Act*. Kathmandu.

68. Gow, (1980, May). *An Information System for the Rural Area Development Rapti Zone Project*. Washington: Development Alternatives, Inc.

69. Hartman, Leigh. (2019, September 23). *What is the U.S. Indo-Pacific Strategy?* ShareAmerica. Retrieved May 8, 2022, from https://share.america.gov/what-is-u-s-indo-pacific-strategy/.

70. HC119. (2016, September 6). *Libya: Examination of intervention and collapse and the UK's future policy options*. House of Commons. Retrieved May 23, 2022, from publications.parliament.uk/pa/cm201617/cmselect /cmfaff/119/119. Pdf

71. Henley, Jon. (2022, May 15). "Finland and Sweden confirm intention to join Nato". *The Guardian*. Retrieved May 18, 2022, from https://www.theguardian.com/world/2022/may/15 /finland-formally-confirms-intention-to-join-nato-russia.

72. Herman, Steve. (2020, January 31). "US-Led Initiative Aims to Make Mark on Global Infrastructure Development". *VOA*. Retrieved March 18, 2011, from https://www.voanews.com/a/economy-business_us-led-initiative-aims-make-mark-global-infrastructure-development/6183503.html.

73. Hewko, John. (2010). *Millennium Challenge Corporation: Can the Experiment Servive?* Washington: Carnegie Endowment for International Peace.

74. Himal Sanchar. (2022, March 18). *US Air Force aircraft in Kathmandu*. Retrieved April 3. 2022, from himalsanchar.com/us-air-force-aircraft-in-kathmandu/.

75. Himalayan News Service. (2022, February 24). "Is this a Pandora's Box, asks China". *The Himalayan Times*. Kathmandu.

76. *Himalkhabar*. (2022, February 26). "Ke Yamsisilai Samsadbata Anumodanko Byabastha Ameriki Chahanama Rakhiyeko Ho? (Is MCC ratification management approved by the

Parliament in the interest of the USA?)".
Kathmandu. Retrieved May 1, 2022, from
https://www.himalkhabar.com/news/128563.

77. Holland, Steve and Faulconbridge, Guy. (2021,
June 13). *G7 rivals China with grand
infrastructure plan*. Reuters. Retrieved March 9,
2021, from https://www.reuters.com/world/g7-
counter-chinas-belt-road-with-infrastructure-
project-senior-us-official-2021-06-12/.

78. Hornick, Ed. (2010, November 18). "Political
Circus: 'Mission Accomplished' finds a home".
CNN Politics. Retrieved May 21, 2022, from
edition.cnn.com/2010/POLITICS/11/18/political.c
ircus/index.html

79. Hudson, Michael. (2022, February 28). *America
Defeats Germany for the Third Time in a Century*.
Retrieved May 19, 2022, from https://michael-
hudson.com/2022/02/america-defeats-germany-
for-the-third-time-in-a-century/.

80. Hughes, Geraint. (2014). *My Enemy's Enemy:
Proxy Warfare in International Politics*. Brighton:
Sussex Academic Press.

81. *Indo-Pacific Strategy of the United States of
America*. (2022, February). Washington: The
White House.

82. Inotal, Andras. (2009, Autumn). *BUDAPEST -
Ghost of second-class status haunts central and
eastern Europe*. Debating Europe.eu. Retrieved
May 17, 2022, from
www.europesworld.org/NewEnglish/Home_old/A
rticle/tabid/191/ArticleType/articleview/ArticleID
/21480/language/en-US/Default.aspx.

83. Joshi, Hemanta. (2022, April 3). "Pancheshwor: Nepal Samjhairahanchha, Bharat Birsihalchha (Pancheshwar: Nepal keeps reminding, India forgets)". *Kantipur*. Kathmamndu: Kantipur Media Group.

84. Karn, Priyanjali. (2022, May 29). "Bhim Bahadur Rawal: MCC compact was steamrolled by ignoring national interest". *The Annapurna Express*. Kathmandu.

85. Karunungan, Lilian. (2022, April 7). "Sri Lanka Faces Wall of Debt Payments Amid Economic Meltdown". *Bloomberg*. Retrieved May 4, 2022, from www.bloomberg.com/news/articles/2022-04-07/sri-lanka-faces-wall-of-debt-payments-amid-economic-meltdown.

86. Keane, Daniel and Blake, Elly. (2022, March 14). "What is the Homes for Ukraine refugees scheme and how do you apply?" *Evening Standard*. Retrieved May 19, 2022, from https://www.standard.co.uk/news/uk/host-ukraine-refugee-scheme-uk-london-russia-war-apply-b987910.html

87. Kelly, Renee. (2015, December 17). *MCC Board Selects Five Countries for MCC Partnerships*. Press Release. Washington: MCC.

88. Kenya Proposed Threshold Program. Retrieved April 1, 2022, from www.mcc.gov/where-we-work/program/kenya-proposed-threshold-program.

89. Khabarhub. (2022, February 10). *US Assistant Secretary of State Donald Lu discusses MCC with Nepal's political leaders over phone*. Kathmandu. Retrieved April 1, 2022, from https://english.khabarhub.com/2022/10/236668/.

90. *Khabarhub*. (2022, February 23). "China sees US-backed MCC Compact as coercive diplomacy in Nepal". Kathmandu. Retrieved May 25, 2022, from https://english.khabarhub.com/2022/23/238625/

91. *Khabarhub*. (2022, March 14). "United States has not threatened Nepal's political leaders on MCC: US Embassy". Kathmandu. Retrieved April 3, 2022, from https://english.khabarhub.com/2022/14/237268/

92. Khatri, Paunab S. (2020, August 9). "BRI and Trans-Himalayan Connectivity". *Nepali Times*. Kathmandu. Retrieved March 21, 2022, from www.nepalitimes.com/latest/bri-and-trans-himalayan-connectivity/.

93. Kimball, Jill. (2021, September 1). "Costs of the 20-year war on terror: $8 trillion and 900,000 deaths". *Watson Institute for International and Public Affairs*. Brown University. Retrieved May 22, 2022, from https://www.brown.edu/news/2021-09-01/costsofwar.

94. Kirby, Paul. (2022, May 9). "Why has Russia invaded Ukraine and what does Putin want?" *BBC News*. Retrieved May 19, 2022, from https://www.bbc.com/news/world-europe-56720589.

95. Kumar, Mayank. (2021, October 2). "China's BRI faces major resistance in Nepal". *Sunday Guardian*. New Delhi. Retrieved April 18, 2022, from www.sundayguardianlive.com/news/chinas-bri-faces-major-resistance-nepal.

96. Kuo, Lily and Kommenda, Niko. (2018, July 30). "What is China's Belt and Road Initiative?" *The*

Guardian. Retrieved March 3, 2022, from https://www.theguardian.com/cities/ng-interactive/2018/jul/30/what-china-belt-road-initiative-silk-road-explainer.

97. Kuo, Mercy A. (2020, April 7). "Blue Dot Network: The Belt and Road Alternative". *The Diplomat*. Retrieved May 9, 2022, from https://thediplomat.com/2020/04/blue-dot-network-the-belt-and-road-alternative/.

98. Lama, Chhapal. (2022, March 20). "Limima chunav Aginai chuniye pratinidhi (Representatives elected in Limi before the elections)". *ekantipur.com*. Retrieved March 20, 2022, from https://ekantipur.com/news/2022/03/20/16477405 16443249.html.

99. Libya Crisis. (2021, March 15). "Libya country profile". *BBC News*. Retrieved May 23, 2022, from www.bbc.com/news/world-africa-13754897

100. LRI. (Undated). *Interpretative Declaration and International Law*. Retrieved April 9, 2022, from https://legalresponse.org/legaladvice/interpretative-declarations-and-international-law/.

101. Lynch, Suzanne. (2013, February 11). "Door is open for Ireland to join Nato, says military alliance's chief". *The Irish Times*. Retrieved May 18, 2022, from www.irishtimes.com/news/door-is-open-for-ireland-to-join-nato-says-military-alliance-s-chief-1.1251258

102. Mahat, Ram Saran. (2021, August 26). "Ratification Imperative for MCC Compact Agreement". *The Kathmandu Post*. Kathmandu: Kantipur Media Group.

103. MCC. (2020, May 7). *Honduras Closed Compact.* Washington.

104. MCC. (2021, September 8). *Response to the Government of Nepal's September 3, 2021, Letter Requesting Clarifications on the MCC Nepal Compact.* Washington.

105. MCC. (2022, January). *Grant Threshold Program Agreement between the MCC and Solomon Islands.* Washington.

106. *MCC.* Retrieved March 30, 2022, from www.mcc.gov/where-we-work.

107. *Millennium Challenge Act of 2003.* (2003). Washington. Retrieved April 7, 2022, from https://www.mcc.gov/resources/doc/millennium-challenge-act-of-2003-amended.

108. *Millennium Challenge Compact Signed Between The United States of America and The Federal Democratic Republic of Nepal.* (2017, September). Washington DC.

109. Millennium Challenge Corporation. (2021, September 8). *Response to the Government of Nepal's September 3, 2021, Letter Requesting Clarification on the MCC Nepal* Compact. Washington.

110. *Millennium Challenge Corporation.* Retrieved April 8, 2022, from www.mcc.gov/about.

111. Millennium Challenge Corporation. Retrieved March 24, 2022, from https://www.mcc.gov/.

112. Ministry of Foreign Affairs Nepal. (2019, October 13). *Joint Statement Between Nepal and the People's Republic of China.* Kathmandu.

113. Ministry of Foreign Affairs. (2022, March 27). *Wang Yi Holds Talks with Nepali Foreign Minister Narayan Khadka*. The People's Republic of China. Retrieved April 14, 2022, from https://www.fmprc.gov.cn/mfa_eng/wjb_663304/wjbz_663308/activities_663312/202203/t20220327_10656332.html.

114. Mount, Mike. (2012, September 21). "U.S. official: Afghanistan surge over as last of extra troops leave country". *CNN*. Retrieved May 22, 2022, from edition.cnn.com/2012/09/20/world/asia/afghanistan-us-troops/index.html.

115. NATO. (2022, January 27). *NATO-Russia relations: the facts*. Brussels.

116. NATO. (2022, March 11). *Relations with Ukraine*. Retrieved May 16, 2022, from www.nato.int/cps/en/natohq/topics_37750.htm.

117. NATO. (2022, March 2). *NATO Response Force units arrive in Romania*. Retrieved May 18, 2022, from https://www.nato.int/cps/en/natohq/news_192695.htm

118. NATO. (2022, May 14). *Enlargement and Article 10*. Brussels. Retrieved May 16, 2022, from https://www.nato.int/cps/en/natolive/topics_49212.htm.

119. NATO. (2022, May 14). *Membership Action Plan (MAP)*. Retrieved May 17, 2022, from https://www.nato.int/cps/en/natolive/topics_37356.htm.

120. NATO. (2022, May 18). *Finland and Sweden submit applications to join NATO*. Brussels. Retrieved May 18, 2022.

121. NDTV. (2022, March 20). *The US' Indo-Pacific Strategy As "Dangerous" As NATO Expansion Near Russia, Says China*. New Delhi. Retrieved March 21, 2022, from https://www.ndtv.com/world-news/us-indo-pacific-strategy-as-dangerous-as-nato-expansion-resulting-in-ukraine-crisis-china-2832518.

122. Nedopil, Christoph (2022). *Countries of the Belt and Road Initiative. Green Finance and Development Center*. Shanghai: FISF Fudan University.

123. *Nepal Live Today*. (2021, September 8). MCC responds to the letter of Nepal government. Retrieved May3, 2022, from www.nepallivetoday.com/2021/09/08/mcc-responds-to-the-letter-of-nepal-government/

124. Nepal, Rosan S. (2019, May 15). "MCC important initiative under Indo-Pacific Strategy". *The Himalayan Times*. Kathmandu. Retrieved May 15, 2019, from https://thehimalayantimes.com/nepal/millennium-challenge-corporation-compact-programme-important-initiative-under-indo-pacific-strategy.

125. *New Spotlight Online*. (2022, April 23). "US Congressional Delegation In Nepal". Retrieved June 1, 2022, from https://www.spotlightnepal.com/2022/04/23/us-congressional-delegation-nepal/.

126. *New Spotlight Online*. (2022, May 7). "It Is In Nepal's Best Interest To Stay Out Of The US' Geopolitical Games: China Daily Editorial".

Retrieved May 19, 2022, from https://www.spotlightnepal.com/2022/03/07/it-nepals-best-interest-stay-out-us-geopolitical-games-china-daily-editorial/.

127. NEWS Africa. (2022, May 23). "Muammar Gaddafi: How he died". *BBC News*. Retrieved May 23, 2022, from www.bbc.com/news/world-africa-15390980.

128. News. (2008, January 23). *Study: Bush led U.S. to war on 'false pretenses'*. Retrieved May 20, 2022, from www.nbcnews.com/id/wbna22794451.

129. *North Atlantic Treaty Organization*. Retrieved May 18, 2022, from https://www.nato.int/cps/fr/natohq/declassified_1 81434.htm.

130. Norton, Ben. (2016, September 16). "U.K. Parliament report details how NATO's 2011 war in Libya was based on lies". Salon. Retrieved May 23, 2022, from U.K. Parliament report details how NATO's 2011 war in Libya was based on lies.

131. Ojeda, Richard. (2021, August 15). The United States spent "2 trillion dollars to train and equip the Afghan military over the past 20 years. They fell in a week."*Politifact*. Retrieved May 22, 2022, from www.politifact.com/factchecks/2021/sep/21/richa rd-ojeda/did-us-spend-2-trillion-support-afghan-military/.

132. *On Development: Nepal Compact Ratification*. Retrieved April 28, 2022, from www.mcc.gov/news-and-events/podcast/episode-033122-nepal-compact-ratification.

133. *Onlinekhabar*. (2020, February 22). "NCP task force tells party not to endorse MCC deal without amendment". Kathmandu. Retrieved on May 1, 2022, from https://english.onlinekhabar.com/ncps-task-force-tells-party-not-to-endorse-mcc-deal-without-amendment.html.

134. Osmańczyk, Jan Edmund. (2002). *Encyclopedia of the United Nations and International Agreements*. Abingdon: Routledge Books.

135. Pach, Chester. (2006, March 2006). "The Reagan Doctrine: Principle, Pragmatism, and Policy". *Presidential Studies Quarterly*. Doi.org/10.1111/j.1741-5705.2006.00288.x

136. Panda, Ankit. (2019, June 11). "The 2019 US Indo-Pacific Strategy Report: Who is it for?" *The Diplomat*. Arlington. Retrieved May 27, 2022, from thediplomat.com/2019/06/the-2019-us-indo-pacific-strategy-report-whos-it-for/.

137. Pande, Jagannath P. (2019, November 4). *Xi's Nepal Visit Reveals a Grander Chinese Himalayan Approach*. New Delhi: Manohar Parrikar Institute for Defence Studies and Analyses.

138. Pandey, Jagadiswar. (2022, February 24). "Nepal Mamilama 'Chinko Baddochaso' (Growing 'Chinese Interest' in Nepal". *Kantipur*. Kathmandu: Kantipur Media Group.

139. Pandey, Jagadishwar. (2022, February 12). "Ameriki Sahayak Bideshamantriko Avibyaktimathi Prashna (Question on saying of the US Assistant Secretary of State)". *Kantipur*. Kathmandu: Kantipur Media Group.

140. Pandey, Jagadishwar. (2022, February 12). "MCCma Kasari Thapio Anumodanko Prawadhan (How added the approval provision in the MCC?)". *Kantipur*. Kathmandu: Kantipur Media Group.

141. Pandey, Jagadiswar. (2021, September 4). "Bibadit 11 Bisaya Prastaparna Amsisilai Patra (Letter of MCC to clarify 11 disputed issues)". *Kantipur*. Kathmandu: Kantipur Media Group.

142. Pant, Anoushka. (2021, August 30). "Right to reject: To vote or not to vote". *The Himalayan Times*. Retrieved June 3, 2022, from thehimalayantimes.com/opinion/right-to-rejectto-vote-or-not-to-vote.

143. Paquette, Laure. (2000). *A Report to the NATO Academic Forum for 1998-2000*. Brussels. Retrieved May 18, 2022, from https://www.nato.int/acad/fellow/98-00/paquette.pdf.

144. Paris Agreement. (2015). *United Nations Framework Convention on Climate Change*. United Nations.

145. Parks, Bradley. (2019, April 1). *Where has the Millennium Challenge Corporation succeeded and failed to incentivize reform—and why?* Brookings. Retrieved March 25, 2022, from https://www.brookings.edu/blog/future-development/2019/04/01/where-has-the-millennium-challenge-corporation-succeeded-and-failed-to-incentivize-reform-and-why/.

146. Patak, Bishnu. (2013, September). "Origin and development of human security". *International Journal of Social and Behavioural Sciences* Vol. 1 (9). Retrieved April 25, 2022, from

http://www.academeresearchjournals.org/journal/i
jsbs.

147. Pathak, Bishnu. (2005). *Politics of People's War
and Human Rights in Nepal*. Kathmandu:
BIMIPA Publications.

148. Pathak, Bishnu. (2008, May 8). "Nepal's 2008
Constituent Assembly Elections: Converting
Bullets to Ballots". *Asia-Pacific Bulletin*.
Washington: East-West Center. Retrieved April
20, 2022, from
https://www.eastwestcenter.org/publications/nepal
s-2008-constituent-assembly-elections-
converting-bullets-ballots.

149. Pathak, Bishnu. (2013, August). "Origin and
development of human security". *International
Journal of Social and Behavioural Sciences*.
Volume 1 (9).

150. Pathak, Bishnu. (2013, February). "Concepts and
Major Initiatives of Human Security".
Contemporary Sociological Global Review.
Volume 3(3). Doi:10.6040/s2027-7431.38118x.

151. Pathak, Bishnu. (2014). "Human Security and
Human Rights: Harmonious to Inharmonious
Relations". *Archives of Business Research*. Vol.2,
No.1.   DOI: 10.14738/abr.21.145.

152. Pathak, Bishnu. (2014). Human Security and
Human Rights: Harmonious to Inharmonious
Relations. Archives of Business Research – Vol.2,
No.1.

153. Pathak, Bishnu. (2015). "Impacts of India's
Transit Warfare against Nepal". *World Journal of
Social Science Research*. Volume 2 (2).

154. Pathak, Bishnu. (2020). "Critiques on the Tribunals and The Hague Court". *Advances in Social Sciences Research Journal.* Vol.7, No.7. DOI:10.14738/assrj.77.8636.

155. *People's Review.* (2021, December 26). "Voce should be raised strongly against MCC: Bhim Rawal". Kathmandu: Periwinkle Prakashan.

156. Peter, Laurence. (2014, September 3). "Why NATO-Russia relations soured before Ukraine". *BBC News.* Retrieved May 18, 2022, from www.bbc.com/news/world-europe-29030744.

157. Pitts, Chip. (2006, August 11). *The Election on Empire.* International Interest Online. Retrieved May 20, 2022, from www.nationalinterest.org/Article.aspx?id=12930.

158. Post Report. (2022, February 20). "Government tables MCC compact in Parliament". *The Kathmandu Post.* Kathmandu: The Kantipur Media Group.

159. Post Reporter. (2021, July 27). "US Secretary of State Antony Blinken calls Prime Minister Sher Bahadur Deuba". *The Kathmandu Post.* Kathmandu: Kantipur Media Group.

160. Poudyal, Biranchi. (2019). "Economic Prospect of Belt and Road Initiatives in Nepal". *KMC Journal.* Kathmandu: Research Department of Koteshwor Multiple Campus.

161. Powell, Anita. (2021, November 4). *"'Build Back Better World': Biden's Counter to China's Belt and Road".* VOA. Retrieved March 18, 2022, from www.voanews.com/a/build-back-better-world-biden-s-counter-to-china-s-belt-and-road/6299568.html.

162. Pradhan, Tika R. (2020, February 21). "Task force advises government not to endorse MCC in current form". *The Kathmandu Post*. Kathmandu: Kantipur Media Group.

163. Press Release. (2010, May 20). *MCC Board Authorizes Termination of Program with Madagascar*. Retrieved March 28, 2022, from https://www.mcc.gov/news-and-events/release/release-051909-mccboardauthorizes.

164. Press Statement. (2017, July 21). *MCC Delegates Visit Nepal to Advance Compact Proposal*. Washington: MCC Headquarters. Retrieved April 1, 2022, from https://www.mcc.gov/news-and-events/release/release-072117-mcc-delegation-nepal.

165. Public Debt Management Office. (2021). *Yearly Report of Nepal Government's Public Debt*. Kathmandu: Nepal Government //pdmo. gov.np/noticedetail/84/2021/50914091.

166. Pun, S.B. (2011, January). "Pancheshwar Multipurpose Project: Nepal's Portion of Water." *HydroNepal*. Issue 9.

167. Quintal, Vanessa. (2021, May 23). *The Belt and Road Initiative: Its Common Destiny and Criticism*. Peace for Asia. Retrieved March 19, 2022, from https://peaceforasia.org/the-belt-and-road-initiative-its-common-destiny-and-criticism/.

168. Rajagopalan, Rajeswari P. (2022, February 25). "Why is the Indo-Pacific Important for Europe". *The Diplomat*. Retrieved March 21, 2022, from https://thediplomat.com/2022/02/why-is-the-indo-pacific-important-for-europe/.

169. Ranjan, Amit. (2021, August 2). *Kathmandu's Closer Ties with Washington: Some Concerns for Beijing*. New Delhi: Institute of South Asian Studies.

170. Ranjan, Amit. (2021, September 20). *The MCC Nepal Compact A Victim of Political Divisions*. Institute of South Asian Studies. National University of Singapore. Retrieved May 1, 2022, from www.isas.nus.edu.sg/papers/the-mcc-nepal-compact-a-victim-of-political-divisions/.

171. Report No. M-000-12-003-S. (2011, March 30). *Review of the Compact Closedout in Nicaragua*. Washington: Office of the Audit for the Millennium Challenge Corporation. Retrieved March 29, 2022, from….

172. Republica. (2021, September 12). "MCC Vice President Sumar leaving Nepal today". *myRepublica*. Kathmandu: Nepal Republic Media.

173. Republica. (2022, February 25). "Khanal warns it will be disastrous if govt passes MCC". *myRepublica*. Kathmandu: Nepal Republic Media.

174. *rfa (Radio Free Asia)*. (2021, June 23). "Asian Countries Welcome G7's Answer to China's One Belt, One Road Program". Retrieved May 9, 2022, from www.rfa.org/english/news/china/program-06232021151152.html.

175. *RFA*. (2021, June 23). "Asian Countries Welcome G7's Answer to China's One Belt, One Road Program". Retrieved March 9, 2022, from https://www.rfa.org/english/news/china/program-06232021151152.html.

176. Rieffel, Lex and Fox, James W. (2008). *Millennium Challenge Corporation: An Opportunity for the next President.* Global Economy and Development Working Paper 30. The Brookings Institution.

177. Romano, David. (2010). "Iraqi Kurdistan: Challenges of Autonomy in the Wake of US Withdrawal". *International Affairs.* Volume 86 (6).

178. Rose, Sarah. (2017, August 11). *MCC has a corruption problem.* Center for Global Development. Retrieved May 28, 2022, from https://www.cgdev.org/blog/mcc-has-corruption-problem.

179. Samaranayaka, DNR. (2020, March 4). "The Dangers Of The Millennium Challenge Corporation Agreement". *Colombo Telegraph.* Retrieved May 28, 2022, from https://www.colombotelegraph.com/index.php/the-dangers-of-the-millennium-challenge-corporation-agreement/.

180. Samaranayake, Nilanthi. (2021, March 2). "Chinese Belt and Road Investment Isn't All Bad—or Good". *FP.* Retrieved March 21, 2022, from https://foreignpolicy.com/2021/03/02/sri-lanka-china-bri-investment-debt-trap/.

181. Sanchez, W. Alejandro. (2013, January 9). "Moldova and NATO: Expansion Stops at the Dniester River? *E-International Relations.* Retrieved May 18, 2022, from https://www.e-ir.info/2013/01/09/moldova-and-nato-expansion-stops-at-the-dniester-river/.

182. SC/7777. (2003, June 5). *UN Inspectors Found No Evidence of Prohibited Weapons Programmes as of 18 March Withdrawal, Hans Blix Tells Security Council*. United Nations. Retrieved May 21, 2022, from www.un.org/press/en/2003/sc7777.doc.htm.

183. Sengupta, Somini. (2006, April 25). "In a Retreat, Nepal's King Says He Will Reinstate Parliament". *The New York Times. New York.*

184. Service, Robert. (2015). *The End of the Cold War: 1985-1991*. Macmillan.

185. Sharma and Neupane. (2022, February 16). "Gathabandhanma Feri Matved (Difference again in the Coalition Partner)". *Kantipur*. Kathmandu: Kantipur Media Group.

186. Sharma, Babita. (2021, December 20). "Yemsisi Samsadma Laijanebare Gathabandanmai Kura Milen (Alliance did not agree submitting the MCC at the Parliament)". *Kantipur*. Kathmandu: Kantipur Media Group.

187. Sharma, Babita. (2022, February 11). "MCC Anumodan Navaye Nepal Nitima Punar Bichar Garne Americako Chetawani (US warns to reconsider Nepal policy if MCC not ratify)". *Kantipur*. Kathmandu: Kantipur Media Group.

188. Sharma, Bhadra. (2020, February 22). "No endorsement of MCC without revisions: NCP panel report". *myRepublica*. Kathmandu: Nepal Republic Media.

189. Shrestha, Bihari K. (2022, February 16). "MCC in the Indo-Pacific Strategy". *People's Review*. Retrieved May 27, 2022, from

www.peoplesreview.com.np/2022/02/16/mcc-in-the-indo-pacific-strategy/.

190. Shrestha, Harsheeta. (2021, December 2). "BRI: A Movement towards Development or A Debt Trap for Nepal ?" *Aidia*. Retrieved March 17, 2022, from http://aidiaasia.org/research-article/bri-a-momentum-towards-development-or-a-debt-trap-for-nepal.

191. Shrestha, Prithvi M & Giri, Anil. (2021, September 8). "MCC responds to Nepal's concerns ahead of its top officials' arrival". *The Kathmandu Post*. Kathmandu: Kantipur Media Group.

192. Skerry, Christa A., Moran, Kerry, and Calavan, Kay M. (1992). *Four Decades of Development: The History of U.S. Assistance to 451 Nepal 1951-1991*. Kathmandu: USAID Nepal.

193. Skobalski, Sergio. (2021, December 23). "Can the G-7's B3W Initiative Compete With China in Latin America?" *The Diplomat*. Retrieved March 1, 2022, from https://thediplomat.com/2021/12/can-the-g-7s-b3w-initiative-compete-with-china-in-latin-america/.

194. Smith, Meagan and Zeigler, Sean M. (2017). "Terrorism before and after 9/11 – a more dangerous world?" *Research and Politics*. Doi: 10.1177/2053168017739757 journals.sagepub.com/home/rap

195. Smith, Stephen. (2021, February 16). "China's Major Country Diplomacy". *Foreign Policy Analysis*. doi:10.1093/fpa/orab002.

196. *South China Morning Post*. (2021, June 12). "G7 leaders adopt 'Build Back Better World' plan to rival China's belt and road strategy". Retrieved May 9, 2022, from https://www.scmp.com/news/world/europe/article/3137097/g7-leaders-adopt-build-back-better-world-plan-rival-chinas-belt.

197. Srinivasan, Chandrashekar. (2022, April 12). "Sri Lanka to default on external debt of $51 billion pending IMF bailout". *Hindustan Times*. New Delhi. Retrieved April 16, 2022, from https://www.hindustantimes.com/world-news/sri-lanka-crisis-sri-lanka-to-default-on-all-external-debt-report-101649745741281.html.

198. *Tanzania Proposed Compact*. Retrieved March 30, 2022, from www.mcc.gov/where-we-work/program/tanzania-proposed-compact.

199. Tarnoff, Curt. (2010, November 16). *Millennium Challenge Corporation*. CRS Report for Congress. Congressional Research Service.

200. Thapa, Bipana. (2019, September 12). "Ambassador Khatri takes initiative to revive 'Nepal caucus' in Washington". *MyRepublica*. Kathmandu. Retrieved April 19, 2022, from https://myrepublica.nagariknetwork.com/news/no-change-on-govt-s-stance-on-bri-indo-pacific-strategy-baskota/.

201. The Department of Defense. (2019, June 1). *Indo-Pacific Strategy Report: Preparedness, Partnership, and Promoting a Network Region*. Washington. Retrieved May 27, 2022, from media.defense.gov/2019/Jul/01/2002152311/-1/-1/1/DEPARTMENT-OF-DEFENSE-INDO-PACIFIC-STRATEGY-REPORT-2019.PDF.

202. *The Economist*. (2020, June 4). "The pandemic is hurting China's Belt and Road Initiative: How will Xi Jinping's biggest project survive?"

203. *The MCC*. Retrieved Aril 28, 2022, from https://www.mcc.gov/about.

204. *The New York Times*. (2006, April 25). "Opposition calls off protests in Nepal". New York. Retrieved April 8, 2022, from www.nytimes.com/2006/04/25/world/asia/opposition-calls-off-protests-in-nepal.html.

205. *The Washington Times*. (2006, August 6). *White House: 'War on terrorism' is over*. Retrieved May 21, 2022, from www.washingtontimes.com/news/2009/aug/6/white-house-war-terrorism-over/.

206. The White House. (2001, January 31). *President Bush Meets with Prime Minister Blair*. Washington. Retrieved May 20, 2022, from georgewbush-whitehouse.archives.gov/news/releases/2003/01/20030131-23.html.

207. The White House. (2003, March 22). "President Discusses Beginning of Operation Iraqi Freedom". *Operation Iraqi Freedom*. Washington. Retrieved May 21, 2022, from georgewbush-whitehouse.archives.gov/news/releases/2003/03/20030322.html.

208. The White House. (2021, June 12). Fact Sheet: President Biden and G7 Leaders Launch Build Back Better World (B3W) Partnership. Retrieved March 9, 2021, from https://www.whitehouse.gov/briefing-room/statements-releases/2021/06/12/fact-sheet-

president-biden-and-g7-leaders-launch-build-back-better-world-b3w-partnership/.

209. The World Bank. (2019, March 29). *Belt and Road Initiative*. Washington.

210. THT Online. (2018, June 21). "Nepal, China sign trade and transit MoUs and agreements". The Himalayan Times. Kathmandu. Retrieved April 16, 2022, from https://thehimalayantimes.com/kathmandu/nepal-china-sign-14-agreements-under-trade-and-transit-agreement

211. U.S. Embassy in Nepal. (2021, September 9). *MCC Vice President Fatema Sumar Visits Nepal*. Kathmandu. Retrieved May 3, 2022, from np.usembassy.gov/media-note-mcc-vice-president-fatema-sumar-visits-nepal/.

212. U.S. Embassy in Nepal. (2022, March 3). *The MCC-Nepal Compact Top Ten Facts*. Kathmandu. Retrieved April 8, 2022, from np.usembassy.gov/mcc-in-nepal-top-ten-facts/.

213. Ukraine-Russia War. (2022, February). "Nord Stream 2: How does the pipeline fit into the Ukraine-Russia crisis?" *BBC News*. Retrieved May 22, 2022, from https://www.bbc.com/news/world-europe-60131520

214. *UN Document: Development*. Retrieved April 8, 2022, from https://research.un.org/en/docs/dev/2000-2015.

215. *Understanding NATO*. Retrieved May 17, 2022, from www.nato.int/docu/presskit/010219/004gb.pdf.

216. UNGS. (2011). Report of the International Law Commission. New York: United Nations.

217. UNHCR. (2022, May 19). *Ukraine Refugees Situation*. Retrieved May 19, 2022, from https://en.wikipedia.org/wiki/2022_Russian_invas ion_of_Ukraine#cite_note-UNHCR-Ukraine-21.

218. United Nations. (2011). Guide to Practice on Reservations of Treaties. New York.

219. UPI. (2013, November 26). "Swiss envoy: Serbia doesn't need to join NATO". Retrieved May 17, 2022, from https://www.upi.com/Top_News/Special/2013/11/26/S wiss-envoy-Serbia-doesnt-need-to-join-NATO/20211385442120/?u3L=1.

220. US Air Force aircraft in Kathmandu. Retrieved April 22, 2022, from https://himalsanchar.com/us-air-force-aircraft-in-kathmandu/.

221. US Department of State. (2021, July 27). *Secretary Blinken's Call with Nepali Prime Minister of Nepal*. Washington. Retrieved May 2, 2022, from www.state.gov/secretary-blinkens-call-with-nepali-prime-minister-deuba/.

222. *US Department of State*. (2022, May 16). "Under Secretary Zeya's travel to India and Nepal". Retrieved May 26, 2022, from https://www.state.gov/under-secretary-zeyas-travel-to-india-and-nepal/.

223. US Department of State. *Blue Dot Network*. Retrieved March 18, 2022, from www.state.gov/blue-dot-network.

224. US Embassy in Nepal. (2020, June 29). *U.S. Embassy Statement on the Millennium Challenge Corporation Compact with Nepal*.

Kathmandu. Retrieved May 2, 2022, from
np.usembassy.gov/u-s-embassy-statement-on-the-
millennium-challenge-corporation-compact-with-
nepal/.

225. Varma, KJM. (2022, February 28). "Irked by
Nepalese Parliament approval to MCC, China
asks US to respect Nepal's sovereignty". *The
Print*. theprint.in/world/irked-by-nepalese-
parliament-approval-to-mcc-china-asks-us-to-
respect-nepals-sovereignty/852135.

226. Vine, David; Coffman, Cala; Khoury, Katalina;
Lovasz, Madison; Bush, Helen; Leduc, Rachael;
and Walkup, Jennifer. (2021, August 19).
"Creating Refugees: Displacement Caused by the
United States' Post-9/11 Wars". *Watson Institute
for International and Public Affairs*. Brown
University.

227. Wagle, Achyut. (2022, February 28). "MCC
through, with a Chinese shadow". *The Kathmandu
Post*. Kathmandu: Kantipur Media Group.

228. Wenbin, Wang. (2022, February 18). "Foreign
Ministry Spokesman's Remarks". *Xinhua News
Agency*. Retrieved April 3, 2022, from
http://kh.china-
embassy.org/eng/fyrth_3/202202/t20220218_106
43446.htm.

229. Westcott, Ben and Ganf, Nanlin. (April 27, 2019).
"China's billion-dollar Belt and Road party: Who's
in and who's out". *CNN*. Retrieved May 5, 2022,
from *edition.cnn.com/2019/04/26/asia/belt-and-
road-summit-beijing-intl/index.html*

230. *Where we work*. Retrieved April 28, 2022, from www.mcc.gov/where-we-work.

231. *Who we select*. Retrieved April 28, 2022, from https://www.mcc.gov/who-we-select.

232. Williams, Brian Glyn. (2012). Innes, Michael (ed.). *Making Sense of Proxy Wars: States, Surrogates and the Use of Force*. Washington DC: Potomac Books.

233. *Xinhua Silk Road Information Service*. (2019, March 15). "Nepali gov't endorses protocol of Nepal-China Transit Transport Agreement: official". Retrieved April 16, 2022, from en.imsilkroad.com/p/133609.html.

234. Xinhua. (2015, March 28). *China unveils action plan on Belt and Road Initiative. The People's Republic of China*. Retrieved May 5, 2022, from english.www.gov.cn/news/top_news/2015/03/28/content_281475079055789.htm.

235. Xuanmin, Li. (2021, July 23). "Xi inspects Tibet, first time in Party's, country's history". *Global Times*. Retrieved May 28, 2022, from www.globaltimes.cn/page/202107/1229449.shtml.

236. Yeping, Yin. (2022, April 14). "Nepal a 'demonstration garden' for friendly cooperation among countries, not a 'fighting ring' for geopolitical games: envoy". *Global Times*. Retrieved April 15, 2022, from https://www.globaltimes.cn/page/202204/125936 3.shtml.

237. Ying. (2017, May 12). "Nepal, China sign bilateral cooperation agreement under Belt and Road Initiative". *Xinhuanet*. Retrieved April 14, 2022, from

http://www.xinhuanet.com/english/2017-05/12/c_136276949.htm

****

www.ingramcontent.com/pod-product-compliance
Lightning Source LLC
Chambersburg PA
CBHW020319290526
45785CB00007B/2845